Corporate Christ is a serious examination of the techniques Jesus used to spread his message, studied from a business perspective. Whatever your beliefs or denomination, there can be no doubt that Jesus' campaign to establish and promote his message was the most successful campaign the world has seen, and businessmen and marketeers the world over have much to learn from his example. It is hoped that readers from all backgrounds and faiths will draw inspiration from this book and the new insights it provides into the life of Christ and the techniques he employed to spread the Word.

CORPORATE CHRIST

For my daughter Lucia

CORPORATE CHRIST

The World-Changing Secrets of a Management and Marketing Genius...

Andrew Finan

First published in Great Britain in 1998 by Management Books 2000 Ltd,
Cowcombe House,
Cowcombe Hill,
Chalford,
Gloucestershire GL6 8HP
Tel: 01285-760722. Fax: 01285-760708
e-mail: MB2000@compuserve.com
web-site: www.mb2000.com

Printed and bound in Great Britain by Biddles, Guildford

British Library Cataloguing in Publication Data is available

ISBN 1-85252-252-6

Acknowledgements

I would like to thank my friends and family for their support. In particular I would like to thank those friends who took part in the photo-shoot for the cover of *Corporate Christ*. Danny King (Chess Grandmaster) deserves a special mention for playing the role of 'Chairman'. Other board members include Warren Standerwick (Architect), John Armstrong (City Trader), Rachel Baxter (Solicitor), Major Johnathan Dyer (Army), Adrian Finn (IT marketer), James Della-Porta (City Trader), Mark Steele (Police Officer), Patrick Skelly (Market Researcher), Brian McGrath (Designer), Simon Smith (Marketing Consultant), Kevin Stewart (Marketing Consultant).

A special thanks to my sister, Lisa, for her enthusiasm and words of encouragement and Rod Alexander for his constructive comments.

Most of all, I wish to thank my wife for her patience and support.

Contents

PART 3. SALES TEAMS, TRAINING AND MOTIVATION

Foreword

At a time when we face ever-mounting social problems, challenges and opportunities, the churches of Britain seem to be bogged down in the mire of committees and bureaucratic structures that paralyse action and prevent real change. In this thought-provoking book, Andrew Finan points us to an older tradition focused on a man who made "the Word become flesh" – not minutes!

Finan helps us to see Jesus of Nazareth with fresh eyes. He challenges us to look, not through the intellectual lenses of the theologian, but through the practical spectacles of the business community. We are helped to see Jesus magnified as an untamed roaring lion rather than the simpering domesticated dog of the traditional Christian church, adored and fussed over by its owners.

Theologians, of course, will remind Finan of the dangers of seeing Jesus through the tinted lenses of our own human experience and history, seeing him simply as a reflection of ourselves. They are right to do so. However, this book makes an important contribution to a church that increasingly will have to come to terms with the fast-moving and ever-changing society in which we now live. The challenges we face in the modern era will demand action rather than talk, leadership rather than consensus, empowerment rather than dependence, faith rather than security. We will need a more people-centred approach that backs those who want to have a go rather than cumbersome original structures that so often stand in the way of growth and progress. Finan reminds us that Jesus chose twelve people whom he empowered and sent out into the world – he did not form a committee...

Reverend Andrew Mawson
Chief Executive, Bromley by Bow Centre
Executive Director, Community Action Centre

Preface

Jesus Christ has had an incalculable impact on the world. His message has dominated the last two millennia and today his followers are counted in their hundreds of millions. More than any other person, Jesus has changed the course of history. His influence reaches deep into the fabric of our society. Law, politics, human rights and culture have all been dramatically affected by the philosophies of this man. He has changed directly or indirectly the lives of billions of people. In his name, solemn oaths have been sworn, monarchs have ruled and wars have been waged. He is arguably the most influential person of all time.

From his origins as the son of a carpenter in a rural town in ancient Israel, he managed to spread his beliefs to the four corners of the world without the aid of mass communication. His message has survived two thousand years and today wins over many thousands of converts to his cause every day.

This level of impact was not achieved by a quirk of history. It was achieved by the extraordinary marketing skills of Jesus Christ. From the start his ambition was to spread the message to the world and he had a clear game plan of how he would achieve it. He meticulously implemented a precise strategy and used stunning management and marketing techniques to achieve his aims. He was a man with a mission and in a hurry. In just three years he set Israel alight with his message and provided the infra-structure for it to continue to spread after his death. Jesus was one of the world's first strategic marketers and can still be regarded as its most successful.

This book does not look at the substance of Jesus' message but how he managed to propagate it. It focuses on the management and marketing genius of the man, his astounding understanding of human psychology and his methods of communication. It uncovers his underlying marketing strategy, how he packaged his message and the extraordinary techniques he used to convey it.

To Christians the impact of Jesus is unsurprising; his Godhead ensured his success. To non-Christians Jesus must still be recognised as a remarkable man, touched by genius, at the very least. Whatever your perspective, the way in which he developed his message merits serious study.

In this book, we take a look at how he selected, motivated and trained disciples as a crack sales force; the sales techniques he used himself and imbued in his disciples; the content and style of his communication; how he handled rejection; how he utilised public relations and conflict to build his name.

It provides a lesson in sales and marketing from the greatest sales person of all time. Anyone who has a vested interest in the business of selling can learn and apply skills used by a man who had complete mastery of them. Step by step, the book shows how Jesus marketed his message and how these systems can be used today.

Introduction

How to use this book

This book is first and foremost about the strategic, marketing and managerial skills of Jesus Christ. Corporate Christ is, therefore, split into three main sections:

1. **Planning and Strategy** – a study of how Jesus applied a strategy to devastating effect. In particular we analyse his last days in Jerusalem and how he planned for the future.

2. **Marketing, Sales and Communication Techniques** – an analysis of the marketing and sales techniques used to spread his message.

3. **Sales Teams, Training and Motivation** – a look at how Jesus selected, instructed, managed and inspired his followers.

Inevitably there are areas of overlap. For instance we will discover that Jesus meticulously planned his recruitment of 'human resources' who in turn played an integral part in the communication and marketing of his message. As in any large corporation, the above areas are not exclusive of each other but inextricably linked. However, dividing the book into three constituent parts makes it easier to comprehend the all round genius of Jesus and his ability to achieve extraordinary feats with limited resources.

What it's not about

This book is not written to pass comment on what Jesus said or did. Neither is it an investigation into the divinity or otherwise of Jesus. There are plenty of other books that address these issues. However, studying Jesus from a 'corporate' perspective does throw a light on a particular side to Jesus that has rarely, if ever, been properly investigated. As I researched into Jesus' 'business acumen', he became a person whom I could understand and identify with – in essence he became more real. It was a very exciting passage of discovery and I hope that as you read this book, you too experience the same excitement as you uncover aspects of the man which had previously been hidden.

Chapter by Chapter – The Wisdom of Jesus

One of the remarkable characteristics of Jesus' life is the frequency with which his actions, decisions and strategies reflect modern marketing techniques. Despite this ancient echo, this book is not written to verify or support modern marketing and management thought. He was unaware of the collective business knowledge that would accrue in the twentieth century and could not have purposefully applied any of the theorems. Furthermore, there were many other occasions when Jesus demonstrated a totally unique approach to marketing and management which is not currently advocated. The success he enjoyed in achieving his ambitions was the result of an instinctive genius, an inner wisdom.

In each chapter, I attempt to unlock that inner wisdom. Concentrating on a specific theme, data is drawn from different sections of the gospels to establish a series of tenets and principles that he lived by. In that respect this book does not pretend to be the A-Z of marketing and management. Instead it provides an insight into one man and his approach. If you agree that this man happened to be a communications and management genius, then who better to have as a role model?

For ease of use, 'Wisdom of Jesus' summaries, which distil the essence of the techniques and skills applied by Jesus, are included at the end of each chapter. These summaries can be treated like 'course notes'. If Jesus was lecturing on a training course today on his experiences and business tenets, I would like to think he would hand out something like these. Readers will find these useful as memory aids and for quick reference.

Original Text

Each chapter deals at some depth with an aspect of Jesus' corporate know-how – be it a marketing technique or an issue of personnel development. Conclusions are backed by quotations from scriptures – not as evidence – but so that the reader can get a 'feel' for the reality of his world by reading the accounts of people who lived in that era. I have predominantly used the King James Version because of its widespread use and its accuracy in translation from the original texts. Often there were an abundance of quotations that could be used to justify particular conclusions but I have avoided doing so. This book was never intended as an academic thesis but rather as a business manual that is both useful and easy to use.

Terminology

The marketing jargon we use today to describe various activities did not exist in the days of Jesus Christ. Jesus would not have spoken of 'building awareness' nor would he describe Christianity as a 'brand'. Jesus used words from two thousand years ago. Marketing then was something you did in a market.

I, on the other hand, do use marketing jargon. It is a more precise vocabulary for talking about marketing in today's context and for that reason I deliberately use modern argot to describe Jesus' managerial and marketing techniques. What Jesus calls 'The Word' or the 'Gospel of the Kingdom' I call the 'message'; when he says 'Spread the Word' I say 'building awareness'. Initially it sounds stilted as you analyse the actions of a person from the ancient world with today's terminology. Ultimately, however, it brings to life the genius of the man as we discover his supreme grasp of marketing and his power to transform and influence the lives of millions of people through the ages.

Supernatural Events

Throughout this book I have avoided comment on supernatural events. Jesus' reputation as a 'wonder-worker' is not an explanation for his modern day fame. In Jesus' time, there were many such wonder-workers accredited with doing equally fantastic deeds who now serve as footnotes in history. Such people were not extraordinary in the Middle-East. In ancient Israel many Jewish wonder-workers of the period healed through the use of magical names. Many rabbis had a reputation for performing miracles including controlling the weather. One such rabbi, Hanina ben Dosa of the late first century AD was believed to be able to cure the sick. Members of another first century Jewish sect called Hasidim were also purported to heal the sick, control the weather and exorcise devils. In themselves, miracles were not particularly remarkable in this period.

What marked Jesus out as arguably the most extraordinary person of all time was not his reputation for miracles but the content of his message and his ability to communicate it.

PART 1

OBJECTIVES, STRATEGY AND PLANNING

1

One Clear Objective

Jesus' Objective

Everything that Jesus said and did was designed to spread his message. He had a special message for the world and he wanted to communicate it. As the Bible reports, he described himself as the 'light of the world', who brought 'good news'. He started his ministry around the Sea of Galilee, but always understood that he needed to take his message to Jerusalem if he was to reach a wider audience. Jesus' whole life was dedicated to the survival of his message and all of his efforts and marketing initiatives we shall be analysing in this book were ultimately driven by this single aim.

Jesus once made clear that he expected the 'Kingdom of God', which he championed, to be like a large tree in which all of the birds could shelter. He saw his ideology reaching wide and deep into society and offering shelter and comfort to many peoples. But he always knew it would not happen overnight. Indeed he knew that it would have very small beginnings – he was never under any misapprehension as to how much work was needed to successfully build his 'Kingdom'. He explained that the start of this new dominion would be just like a seed – and from this would grow the 'Kingdom' of which he preached – *"It is like a grain of mustard seed, which a man took and cast into his garden; and it grew, and waxed a great tree; and the fowls of the air lodged in the branches of it."* (Luke 13:19).

2

Formulating a Strategy

Grand Plans

From the beginning to the end, everything was planned. Jesus waited until he was ready then unleashed himself on an unsuspecting world. He knew from the start what he wanted to achieve and how he would make it happen. And, from beginning to end, it all went to plan.

The series of events which were so radically to shape the world in which we now live were not a series of unconnected, random occurrences but part of the grand strategy of Jesus. Once we establish the framework of his strategy we can see the brilliance of his marketing genius running throughout. This section deals with the implementation of Jesus' overall strategy.

It is to the end of his story that we travel first – the last extraordinary days before Jesus was sentenced to death by the Romans. His demise was the ultimate act in his Jerusalem plan – his swan song in a complex, colourful and dramatic dance of death. As in a great ballet, he built up to the final denouement with consummate skill, drawing the audience in with spectacular gestures and only when he had the crowd completely transfixed, did he allow the tragedy to reach its climax. His time in Jerusalem, therefore, was carefully choreographed, each act laying the groundwork for the next to follow seamlessly. By the end, he had Jerusalem enraptured and the survival of his message was guaranteed.

Strike at the Heart

Jesus always planned that his swan song would be in the capital. For this man, from a small hamlet in Galilee, Jerusalem was the centre of his world and his inevitable destiny lay in it. It was the Jewish centre of culture, politics, trade and religion. Crucially it was the centre of Jewish influence. The individuals and authorities who ran Israel all resided and operated in Jerusalem. It was there that the chief priests, the Sanhedrin[1], the Roman Governor and the often visiting King Herod, all resided in an uneasy coexistence. From these luminaries emanated the power that shaped and influenced people's lives. Jesus knew that in order to have a wide impact, he needed to embroil this Byzantine network of officials into his own grand strategy. He may have started his ministry in Galilee but he knew he would finish in Jerusalem.

Jerusalem

Jerusalem is built on a hill seventy miles south of Galilee, forty east of the Mediterranean and fifteen west of the Dead Sea. It had been the ancient capital of King David about a thousand years before Jesus was born. At the time of Jesus, it was capital of the province of Judea the ancient forerunner of modern Israel and was occupied by Romans who maintained a heavy military presence. They oversaw an indigenous population estimated at 40,000. Many thousands more visited the city from all over the ancient world at the time of the major festivals and in particular at the time of the Passover. Architecturally Jerusalem was a walled city dominated by the Temple which was originally commissioned by King Solomon.

Maximising Impact

Like any major city, Jerusalem was populated by thriving, busy people with day to day concerns, distractions and preoccupations. To 'capture' it, Jesus knew he needed to make a big impact and then retain its attention.

There were four elements to Jesus' strategy in Jerusalem:

Stage 1. Maximise impact on entrance to Jerusalem – become the focal point of attention.

Stage 2. Retain the attention of Jerusalem

Stage 3. Communicate the message.

Stage 4. Ensure the survival of the message.

The tactics he employed to carry out his strategy were radical and ingenious. We will analyse each stage in turn as he moved himself ever closer to his violent destiny.

The gospel writers

There are four gospels included in the bible – those written by Matthew, Mark, Luke and John. It is impossible to give precise dates as to when the gospels were written but many historians agree that they were probably all penned between 60 – 80 AD. The first three gospels – Matthew, Mark and Luke – all have a similar style and content. For that reason they are called the Synoptic Gospels (from the Greek word meaning 'seen together'). Some scholars speculate that Matthew and Luke drew on Mark and another source called Q (from the German 'Quelle' meaning which) but unless Q is ever found it will remain an unproved theory.

(contd)

John has a style distinct from the other gospels. He focuses less on Jesus' actions and deeds and more on his sayings and lengthy discourses. It is probable that John's information came from a different oral tradition.

While each of the synoptic gospels often helps to flesh out a story, John brings a different perspective. It can be compared to reading radically different newspapers, written for different audiences but reporting on the same events. The extra dimension provided by John helps to bring the real Jesus into focus.

The Wisdom of Jesus

1. **Have one clear objective.**

2. **Have a clear vision of your objective. What would it look like to have your ambition fulfilled.**

3. **Plan right through to the delivery of your objective.**

4. **Devise a clear strategy that will deliver your objective.**

5. **Ensure that big gestures are carried on the biggest possible stage.**

3

Stage 1 – Grabbing the Limelight

Gathering Momentum

And he went through the cities and villages, teaching and journeying toward Jerusalem. (Luke 13:22).

Jesus did not rush directly into Jerusalem but took a long route, continually preaching and gaining support along the way. He actually travelled in a large arc around the capital as he covered all the region outside the great city. When he finally reached Jerusalem he organised an entrance that no one would forget – a triumphant entrance – one fit for a king.

Fanfare Entrance

From early on in the scriptures, we know that Jesus had a triumphant entrance into Jerusalem in mind. Jesus, while on his way to the capital, made a passionate outburst that a prophet can not *perish out of Jerusalem* (Luke 13:33) and that the city of Jerusalem would not see him until he was welcomed like a prophet. His preparations to be received as one were painstaking. As a learned scholar he knew, for instance, that it had long been prophesied in the Old Testament book of Zechariah[2] that the Messiah would arrive in Jerusalem on an ass. In order to fulfil that prophecy Jesus made deliberate arrangements to have an ass ready to carry him.

> *And when they drew nigh unto Jerusalem, and were come to Bethphage, unto the mount of Olives, then sent Jesus two disciples, Saying unto them, "Go into the village over against you, and straightway ye shall find an ass tied, and a colt with her: loose them, and bring them unto me. And if any man say ought unto you, ye shall say, 'The Lord hath need of them'; and straightway he will send them." All this was done, that it might be fulfilled which was spoken by the prophet, saying, "Tell ye the daughter of Sion, Behold, thy King cometh unto thee, meek, and sitting upon an ass, and a colt the foal of an ass." (Matthew 21:1-5)*

This almost mundane story reveals much about the historical figure of Jesus. It shows him to be a stickler for detail – a meticulous planner. He knew the location of the village and furthermore knew exactly where the ass and colt were tied. We know he must have arranged to have them ready and probably asked for someone to guard them until his men came to take it. Having secured an appropriately portentous vehicle for entry, Jesus then orchestrated his reception.

> *And a very great multitude spread their garments in the way; others cut down branches from the trees, and strowed them in the way. And the multitudes that went before, and that followed, cried, saying, "Hosanna to the son of David: Blessed is he that cometh in the name of the Lord; Hosanna in the highest." (Matthew 21:8-9)*

Planned reception

Jesus had turned his entry into a victory parade, a huge spectacle with people strewing garments and leaves in his path. Careful study of the text reveals that this was not an impromptu welcome by the residents of Jerusalem (who did not actually know who he was). On the contrary it was the disciples themselves who put on and orchestrated the reception. Along with the procurement of the ass, the whole episode had been meticulously planned.

> *And when he was come nigh, even now at the descent of the mount of Olives, the whole multitude of the disciples began to rejoice and praise God with a loud voice for all the mighty works that they had seen; Saying, "Blessed be the King that cometh in the name of the Lord: peace in heaven, and glory in the highest." (Luke 19:37-38)*

The crowd chanted slogans and strew garments in his path. The saga bears a remarkable resemblance to a New York ticker tape parade or a party convention organised by the US Republican or Democratic parties. Jesus wanted to make a big impact on Jerusalem and his grand entrance was wonderfully effective. The whole of Jerusalem was intrigued and wanted to know who he was. His disciples were on hand to inform them.

> *And when he was come into Jerusalem, all the city was moved, saying, "Who is this?" and the multitude said, "This is Jesus the prophet of Nazareth of Galilee." (Matthew 21:10-11)*

Jesus revelled in and encouraged the festivities. The razzmatazz of the occasion suited his needs. The onlooking Pharisees, however, were disconcerted by the commotion and urged Jesus to instruct his disciples to cease. Jesus snubbed their request – it was all part of his higher plan!

> *And some of the Pharisees from among the multitude said unto him, "Master, rebuke thy disciples." And he answered and said unto them, "I tell you that, if these should hold their peace, the stones would immediately cry out." (Luke 19:39-40)*

Stage 1 of his strategy was complete. Jesus had Jerusalem's attention.

The Pharisees and scribes

The Pharisees and scribes (sometimes referred to as lawyers) were apologists for the Jewish Law. They believed in the absolute adherence to every aspect of the Law down to the tiniest detail. The Law came from two sources: the written Law of Moses and oral traditions handed down through generations. The Pharisees and scribes believed that every deed performed, no matter how trivial, was of interest to God and that there would be a day of judgement when the evil would be cast aside and the righteous would rise up to worship him. Rigorous application of the Law had big implications for everyday life. Rituals for maintaining purity and observing Laws associated with the Sabbath were particularly burdensome for many.

The Wisdom of Jesus

1. **Be patient. Wait for the optimum moment to strike.**
2. **Be meticulous in preparation of an event.**
3. **Grab the limelight.**
4. **Arrange your own receptions.**
5. **Arrive in appropriate style.**
6. **Have supporters on hand to clap and cheer.**
7. **Use items which can be thrown for visual impact.**
8. **Have supporters on hand to explain the message.**
9. **Remember that nothing attracts a crowd like a crowd.**

4

Stages 2 & 3 – Retaining Attention

Violence in the Temple

Jesus had been received like a king into Jerusalem. He was flavour of the day and his name tripped from everyone's lips. But fame in itself was never his ambition. It was simply a means to an end.

Jesus realised the transient nature of his current celebrity. Like any sophisticated metropolis, Jerusalem's chattering classes had a low attention span moving from one fad to the next. Today Jesus, tomorrow someone else. Jesus wanted to be taken more seriously. He wanted to fix attention on himself. Celebrity can be a flighty, ephemeral affair, touching one and then moving to another. We have all witnessed flash-in-the-pans. People who make the headlines for a week and then are gone – hardly causing a ripple in our busy lives except as a mere diversion. Jesus would not allow this to happen to him. He wanted to burn his message into our psyches.

His next act was cold, calculating and devastatingly effective. He marched into the Temple and wrecked it, claiming the holy site had become a den of thieves.

And Jesus went into the temple of God, and cast out all them that sold

> *and bought in the temple, and overthrew the tables of the money-changers, and the seats of them that sold doves, and said unto them, "It is written, 'My house shall be called the house of prayer[3]; but ye have made it a 'den of thieves[4].'" (Matthew 21:12-13)*

It is hard to imagine a more outrageous, dangerous and headline-grabbing stunt. Jerusalem would have been stunned by his antics. One moment he is feted as a king, prophet or messiah, the next he behaves like a delinquent in the Temple.

Modern day observers need to imagine the commotion that would be caused if a foreign dignitary entered the House of Commons or the US Senate and demolished it. It would be headline news. To Jews, the Temple, if anything, was more important than the two illustrious institutions I have just mentioned. It contained the holy of holies and was the centre of Jewish culture and life. By this act, Jesus guaranteed total focus on himself – he was the biggest story in town.

The Temple

We know from Luke's Gospel that as a boy, Jesus travelled frequently to Jerusalem with his parents to attend the religious festivals (Luke 2:41). The Temple, which was the focal point for all Jewish life, could not have failed to impress the boy. Its towering walls, which still stand today, were one of the most impressive sights in the Roman Empire. We know from the first century Jewish historian Flavius Josephus that the scale and opulence of the Temple was a source of wonder for all who witnessed it. Even well travelled Romans, familiar with the grand buildings of Rome, were awe-struck by this construction.

The Temple of Herod consisted of an Inner Sanctum, which was built in the reign of King Solomon, nearly one thousand years before Jesus was born. Around this, King Herod had built a complex of grand scale courts. Visitors had to pass through nine doors from the outer courts to the Inner Sanctum and along the way, inscriptions in Greek and Latin told visitors of the cleansing rituals required if they wished to progress further. They also warned foreigners of trespassing into the holy areas. One such inscription that survives states: "Foreigners are forbidden from entering through the balustrade into the enclosure around the sanctuary. Anyone doing so will be to blame for the death that will follow." Only the chief priest himself was allowed into the Inner Sanctum.

The Jews made ritual offerings of animals or crops inside the Temple courtyards. Different sacrifices were specified in the law for different occasions – one type of sacrifice for thanksgiving another to seek forgiveness, etc. The offerings were burnt on enormous altars by the temple priests. The sacrificial animals needed to be purchased and so there were vendors selling them outside. At the time of festivals, it would undoubtedly have been a roaring trade with a high turnover of cash. However, ritual required that Roman coins with the idolatrous head of Caesar were not brought into the Temple. There were, therefore, money changers who would change Roman money into acceptable currency. It was this commercial trade that Jesus targeted in his rampage – but in many ways it was a necessary activity to enable people to make sacrifices and avoid defiling the Temple.

Pre-meditated Violence

From Matthew's Gospel, we might be left with the impression that this might have been an impulsive act – not planned at all. It would be possible to surmise that Jesus simply lost his temper and self control and in the heat of the moment went into a wild rage. The other gospels, however, flesh out the incident and show that this was a premeditated act of vandalism. A deed completed with astonishingly cool deliberateness. The day before he wrecked it, Jesus made a site visit!

> *And Jesus entered into Jerusalem, and into the temple and when he had looked round about upon all things, and now the eventide was come, he went out unto Bethany with the twelve. (Mark 11:11)*

Jesus had entered and took in the full scene the night before! He *looked round about on all things* and then left. No knee jerk reaction – just calm assessment of the situation before retiring to Bethany, a village close to the city, to contemplate his next move. Mark's Gospel goes on to tell of how he went up to Jerusalem the next day to wreck the Temple. Irrespective of whether Jesus' actions are considered to be justified, the gospels, in black and white give compelling evidence of violent behaviour.

John's gospel gives us even more revealing detail:

> *And the Jews' Passover was at hand, and Jesus went up to Jerusalem, and found in the temple those that sold oxen and sheep and doves, and the changers of money sitting: and when he had made a scourge of small cords, he drove them all out of the temple, and the sheep, and the oxen; and poured out the changers' money, and overthrew the tables; and said unto them that sold doves, "Take these things hence; make not my Father's house an house of merchandise." (John 2:13-16)*

John's account contains explicit depiction of the violence and more evidence of the premeditated nature of the incident – Jesus took time to make a whip! Presumably Jesus made it the night before in Bethany. We can not be sure if he actually harmed anyone with his extreme behaviour but we do know that, such was its impact, this is one of the few stories that is covered by all four gospel writers.

Perfect Timing

Jesus' timing was perfect for impact. During Passover Jerusalem would have been heaving with visitors from all over the Mediterranean and now, following his scandalous behaviour in the Temple, his notoriety was guaranteed to spread across the Empire. His insubordinate actions would have made him enemies – powerful enemies too. Causing a disruption under the nose of the chief priests and the Romans was highly provocative, not to say mortally dangerous.

Educating the people

Jesus left the scene in chaos and coolly headed back to Bethany where he could rest, reflect and plan his next move. Any ordinary man, not intent on putting his life at risk, would have withdrawn from the region and sought sanctuary afar. Jesus was not an ordinary man and was back at the scene of the incident the very next morning preaching and teaching his philosophies and principles.

Stage two and three of his strategy were complete. He had the attention of the people and now they were listening.

Stage four of his strategy was to orchestrate his own death. Jesus literally had a death wish and, as we shall see, he attacked and castigated the authorities until he forced their hand. Jesus fanned the flames of conflict.

The Wisdom of Jesus

1. **Build on transient fame to make a more permanent impact.**

2. **Make your next move while you are still the centre of attention.**

3. **Use shock tactics to retain attention.**

4. **Make a site visit before pulling off a major stunt.**

5. **Consider the impact and consequences of your actions carefully.**

6. **Strike at the heart of cultural life for maximum impact.**

7. **Be controversial.**

8. **Time the event for maximum impact.**

9. **Be prepared for a backlash with the authorities.**

5

Stage 4 – Mission Accomplished

Extreme Provocation

In Tiananmen Square, Beijing, in 1989, a young man involved in pro-democracy demonstrations stood in front of a government tank and brought a Chinese military convoy to a standstill. The pictures of this one man standing up to tyranny were beamed across the world and presented one of the most powerful images of the twentieth century. The young man lived in an oppressive regime and was fully aware that his act would result in imprisonment or possibly death by execution. He was in fact imprisoned for a number of years, and only recently released, in 1998, on the grounds of his deteriorating medical condition.

He wanted to draw attention to the plight of millions of Chinese who sought democracy and freedom. His personal sacrifice was not in vain. His act galvanised world opinion against China's poor human rights record and anti-democratic government. From this viewpoint, his individual stand was stunningly effective – more effective than the lame words of the United Nations and the hitherto weak diplomatic efforts of the Western World.

Two millennia before this incident, Jesus Christ lived under the reign of another oppressive regime and he wanted to sacrifice his life to ensure the establishment of a new moral code. His method, similar to the man who held up the tanks in China, was to provoke the authorities in a highly public confrontation. Jesus understood that by sacrificing himself he could make himself and more importantly his message famous.

Jesus' technique was to needle and provoke the authorities until they had no option but to take drastic action against him. He behaved like a modern day dissident constantly criticising official hypocrisy and corruption. The authorities, desperate to avoid an unseemly spectacle, sought to undermine Jesus and his sect by damaging his credibility. Jesus, however, was a polished politician as well as being a consummate strategist – he knew which buttons to press and they became ever more aggravated. They hatched a series of devious schemes to undermine Jesus but discovered him to be a formidable maverick and more than a match for them. They became ever more desperate. Desperation led to desperate measures and Jesus ultimately pushed them into the use of ultimate force and the signing of his death warrant.

Planning Long Term

To devise such a complex scheme took careful planning. Jesus had been preparing for his trip to Jerusalem and ensuing death for a long time. He had frequently spoken of his intention to go there and be put to death. The Gospels of Matthew and Mark state that on the way to Jerusalem there were at least three occasions when Jesus explained to his disciples that he was going to Jerusalem to be executed by the authorities.

> *Saying, "Behold, we go up to Jerusalem; and the Son of man shall be delivered unto the chief priests, and unto the scribes; and they shall condemn him to death, and shall deliver him to the Gentiles:" (Mark 10:33)*

Despite Jesus' many attempts to explain the reasons for visiting

Jerusalem, the disciples could not grasp the enormity of what Jesus was saying for *they understood none of these things: and this saying was hid from them, neither knew they the things which were spoken.* (Luke 18:31-34)

Undoubtedly Jesus was frustrated by their lack of comprehension. He was convinced that Jerusalem was the key to his success and that all that he had achieved to date would come to nought if he failed there.

> *"Nevertheless I must walk today, and tomorrow, and the day following: for it cannot be that a prophet perish out of Jerusalem." (Luke 13:33)*

For him each day was just another step towards his own violent destiny. Jesus would not contemplate any other option and so sealed his own fate. The utterance confirms that Jesus believed that he, like all the great prophets before him, must die there. For him to die anywhere else was unthinkable. Jerusalem was the platform from which to launch his message to the whole world.

Complete Focus

The successful execution of such an extraordinary plan could not have occurred without the complete commitment of our protagonist to see it through. Throughout his life, Jesus demonstrated courage and an iron will which never deserted him. Even though he knew those days were to be his last, he never flinched from his own self imposed destiny. All his energies were channelled into achieving his objectives. Luke makes his focus on the city clear:

> *And it came to pass, when the time was come that he should be received up, he steadfastly set his face to go to Jerusalem. (Luke 9:51)*

Even when the Pharisees used scare tactics to keep him away from the capital, Jesus remained undaunted. The death that they threatened him with – Jesus already had in mind! *The same day there came certain of the Pharisees, saying unto him, "Get thee out, and depart hence: for HerodKing Herod will kill thee."* (Luke 13:31)

For the disciples, who clearly had little comprehension of Jesus' strategy, the prospect of their leader going to Jerusalem to be put to death was a frightening one. All this talk of death was unsettling and made little sense to them when everything seemed to going so well. Peter took it upon himself to put him straight. The resulting confrontation illustrates Jesus' determination to reach his objective.

> *And he began to teach them, that the Son of man must suffer many things, and be rejected of the elders, and of the chief priests, and scribes, and be killed, and after three days rise again. And he spake that saying openly. And Peter took him, and began to rebuke him. But when he had turned about and looked on his disciples, he rebuked Peter, saying, Get thee behind me, Satan: for thou savourest not the things that be of God, but the things that be of men. (Mark 8:31-33)*

Jesus was incensed by Peter's ignorance and interference. He saw him as an obstacle in the way of him achieving his own death and accused him with being Satan himself. In the context of who Jesus was and what he stood for, he could not have hurled a more abusive insult at his friend and follower.

Jesus had no intention of letting anyone, even one of his followers and closest friends, prevent him from staging his death in Jerusalem. The next day he would have been found nailed to a wooden cross next to two robbers who were also crucified. Jesus was close to his ultimate destiny.

Long Term Strategy

To manoeuvre the authorities to the point where their intentions had turned murderous took years of head-to-head conflict. He nudged them towards the precipice every time he publicly embarrassed or maligned them. It was a long term process which had its origins in the earliest days of his ministry. By studying how the conflict grew from a few isolated spats early in the ministry into full scale verbal warfare, we can discern his long term game plan; appreciate how he slowly notched up the pressure; and comprehend how his world-changing activities in Jerusalem had in fact followed years of groundwork and preparation. Mark recorded an early encounter with the authorities that marked the origins of their long running feud.

> *And he entered again into the synagogue; and there was a man there which had a withered hand. And they watched him, whether he would heal him on the sabbath day; that they might accuse him. And he saith unto the man which had the withered hand "Stand forth" and he saith unto them, "Is it lawful to do good on the sabbath days, or to do evil? To save life, or to kill?" But they held their peace. And when he had looked round about on them with anger being grieved for the hardness of their hearts, he saith unto the man "Stretch forth thine hand." And he stretched it out: and his hand was restored whole as the other. (Mark 3:1-6)*

The tension is palpable. The Pharisees waited in a silent, menacing manner to catch him out. Healing on the Sabbath would be considered to be work and therefore not permissible. Jesus derided it as a petty law which in effect outlawed good deeds on this holy day of the week. He taunted the Pharisees. He was deliberately adversarial, belligerent and controversial. His aggressive manner had dire but not unexpected consequences:

> *... and the Pharisees went forth, and straightway took counsel with the HerodKing Herodians against him, how they might destroy him. (Mark 3:6)*

Verbal Warfare in Jerusalem

Once in Jerusalem the conflict with the authorities reached boiling point. A series of highly public clashes ensued starting with the chief priests.

Round 1 – The chief priests

> *And when he was come into the temple, the chief priests and the elders of the people came unto him as he was teaching and said, By what authority doest thou these things? And who gave thee this authority? (Matthew 21:23)*

In modern day language the authorities asked him just who did he think he was. Jesus had anticipated this opening gambit. He handled it with the guile of a seasoned politician. Instead of answering the question, he set one of his own and snared them in a nasty dilemma:

> *And Jesus answered and said unto them, "I also will ask you one thing, which if ye tell me, I in like wise will tell you by what authority I do these things. The baptism of John, whence was it? From heaven, or of men?" And they reasoned with themselves, saying, "If we shall say, 'From heaven'; he will say unto us, 'Why did ye not then believe him?' But if we shall say, 'Of men'; we fear the people; for all hold John as a prophet." And they answered Jesus, and said, "We cannot tell." And he said unto them, "Neither tell I you by what authority I do these things." (Matthew 21:24 – 27)*

The chief priests, outmanoeuvred and embarrassed by Jesus, withdrew, leaving him the stage. Stung by his criticism and easy victories, the authorities regrouped and planned a series of cunning ruses to exact their revenge. There followed a succession of extraordinary polemical clashes between Jesus and different representatives of the authorities.

Round 2 – Spies

Next the authorities posted spies who pretended to be ordinary members of the public. Their mission was to listen to everything that Jesus said and wait for a misplaced word or comment that could be reported

Basis of Conflict

Although Jesus used his on-going rivalry with the authorities to manipulate events, his opposition to them was not contrived – it was based on fundamental philosophical differences. Parts of Jesus' new philosophy were diametrically opposed to the beliefs of mainstream Judaism and in particular sects such as the Pharisees which adhered to strict application of their religious law in every aspect of their lives. He saw many of their practices as hypocritical, ridiculous and to the detriment of being good to fellow citizens. Jesus symbolised a new religion that was not elitist or dependent on arcane practices but open to everyone who asked for forgiveness. His populist message attracted a wide following and often brought him into contact with unsavoury characters such as tax collectors, zealots and adulterers – types abhorred and despised by the Pharisees.

Beyond the doctrinal differences Jesus had with the Pharisees, the governing authorities worried about Jesus too. His large and fanatical following made him dangerous. They feared his ever growing support would attract unwelcome attention from Rome and result in a heavy crackdown with the authorities forced to forfeit what power they still held.

back to the Roman Governor and used against him. They even attempted to snare Jesus with a loaded question on whether taxes should be paid to Caesar. This was a minefield. The Romans forced crippling taxes on the poor. To be an enthusiastic supporter of these taxes would alienate him from his following which naturally loathed the paying taxes to their Roman overlords. To oppose taxes would give the spies the ammunition they needed. They could inform the governor that Jesus was encouraging tax avoidance. Jesus saw the trap.

> *But he perceived their craftiness, and said unto them, "Why tempt ye me? Show me a penny. Whose image and superscription hath it?" They answered and said, "Caesar's." And he said unto them, "Render therefore unto Caesar the things which be Caesar's, and unto God the*

> *things which be God's." And they could not take hold of his words before the people: and they marvelled at his answer, and held their peace. (Luke 20:20-26)*

The intelligence of Jesus' answer rings down through the centuries. He showed himself to be quick, composed and supremely confident. His assured performances left the authorities flat-footed and ever more desperate.

Round 3 – The Sadducees

The Sadducees were next. Playing the role of educated buffoons, they set an absurdly complex point of law as to whose wife would a woman be after her death if she married many times and then died without child. Jesus brushed the question aside saying the dead will not be married thus treating the question with the contempt it deserved. They had been put in their place and *after that they durst not ask him any question at all.* (Luke 20:40)

Round 4 – The Lawyer

Once the Pharisees had learnt that the Sadducees had been silenced they sent a law specialist who attempted to catch him out with an open question on which was the most important commandment.

> *Jesus said unto him, "Thou shalt love the Lord thy God with all thy heart, and with all thy soul, and with all thy mind. This is the first and great commandment. And the second is like unto it, Thou shalt love thy neighbour as thyself. On these two commandments hang all the law and the prophets." (Matthew 22:37-40)*

Jesus had spoken commendably. The lawyer had failed in his mission.

Round 5 – The Pharisees and knock-out blow

Jesus then posed a question to the Pharisees on who did they think was the Christ (Messiah).

> *While the Pharisees were gathered together, Jesus asked them, saying, "What think ye of Christ? Whose son is he?" They say unto him, "The son of David." He saith unto them, "How then doth David in spirit call him Lord, saying, 'The Lord said unto my Lord, Sit thou on my right hand, till I make thine enemies thy footstool?' If David then call him Lord, how is he his son?" And no man was able to answer him a word, neither durst any man from that day forth ask him any more questions." (Matthew 22:41-45)*

Despite their most devious efforts, the authorities could not defeat Jesus in verbal warfare. He had consistently embarrassed and humiliated them and then, just when their frustration and vulnerability were at their greatest, Jesus launched a devastating volley of criticisms and insults that left the authorities reeling. He humiliated them in front of the crowd. He accused them of being self-important, of pretending to pray, of 'devouring widows' houses', of being full of 'extortion and excess', for being vain, unjust, oppressive, of being unclean and 'full of dead men's bones', of being obsessed with gold and of turning converts into 'children of hell'. He called them 'hypocrites', 'serpents', 'vipers' and labelled them as the descendants of murderers. Jesus could not have been more insulting. He had pushed all the right buttons and knew how they would respond.

Jesus had given a salutary lesson in how to shred the reputation of an adversary. To savour the extreme force of Jesus' withering tirade against the authorities, it is worth reading the full text of Matthew 23:1-37.

The authorities had received a complete mauling by Jesus. The scale, cohesion and precision of Jesus' attack indicates that this was a deliberate, prepared assault, executed for the public benefit. As far as the authorities were concerned, it was an assault too far. They felt compelled to defend themselves against Jesus' vitriolic attack. The time for words was over. They assembled at the palace of the chief priest and *consulted that they might take Jesus by subtlety, and kill him* (Matthew 26:3-4).

Jesus was aware that he had signed his own death warrant. By challenging the authorities he had essentially taken on the state. In ancient Israel, there was no distinction between secular and religious rule – it was all one and the same. He had succeeded in pushing them over the edge. While the authorities all assembled to plot against him, he told his disciples how they would eliminate him.

> *And it came to pass, when Jesus had finished all these sayings, he said unto his disciples, "Ye know that after two days is the feast of the Passover, and the Son of Man is betrayed to be crucified." Then assembled together the chief priests, and the scribes, and the elders of the people, unto the palace of the high priest, who was called Caiaphas, And consulted that they might take Jesus by subtlety, and kill him. (Matthew 26:1-4)*

The Finishing Touch

Jesus continued to pull the strings. He had manipulated the authorities into plotting to kill. He now wanted to control the method of his elimination. For the authorities to 'remove' him quietly by discreetly employing an assassin would have been a disaster for Jesus. In the confusion that would have followed his disappearance, his message would have died with him. His final gesture had to be on the big stage – a sight the whole of Israel would remember.

As a learned man Jesus knew that the Jews were not permitted to condemn a man to death (John 18:31). Only the Romans could do this and they guaranteed a high profile execution. They were vicious, ruthless and subscribed to the policy of making an example of those that dared cross the rule of Rome. Therefore Jesus stage managed his own arrest and ultimate delivery to the Roman Governor who would order his public crucifixion.

Crucifixion

Crucifixion was a particularly gruesome form of execution reserved for those accused of treason against Rome. The perpetrators were nailed to a wooden beam and left to hang naked and exposed. It was often days before they died. This form of capital punishment was used primarily to act as a deterrent to other criminals. The words of a Roman who lived two hundred years after Jesus best describe its purpose:

Whenever we crucify the guilty, the most crowded roads are chosen, where most people can see and be moved by fear. For penalties relate not so much to retribution as to their exemplary effect. (Quintilian Declamationes 274 AD).

Manipulation

Jesus was cognisant that Judas, one of his disciples, was contemplating betraying him. Unfortunately, we do not know how he knew of this scheme – whether he had put the idea into Judas' head or whether he had simply rumbled his intention. Either way he put the knowledge to use.

At what was fated to be Jesus' last meal with his disciples (the Last Supper), Jesus identified Judas as his betrayer and then instructed him to complete the task – fast. *That thou doest, do quickly.* (John 13:27). Judas promptly slipped into the night and met up with the authorities to let them know where they could arrest him. He *knew the place: for Jesus ofttimes resorted thither with his disciples* (John 18:2).

The time was right for events to take their course. Jerusalem was buzzing with talk of Jesus – his fame had hit an all time high. To capitalise on his celebrity, he wanted to his execution to coincide with the Passover, a poignant time for the Jewish nation and a time when Jerusalem was bulging with visitors from all over Israel and beyond.

Passover

The Passover is the great Jewish festival celebrating the liberation of the Jews from slavery in ancient Egypt over 1,000 years before Jesus' birth. The event, which lasted seven days, was a spectacular, vibrant and colourful occasion with choirs, bands, singing, dancing and priests in colourful raiments. Over the Passover, Jews avoid eating bread or leavened foods. The Passover, or 'Passah' as the Jews would call it, brought many thousands of pilgrims to the city every year.

The Last Supper also presented the authorities with a golden opportunity. They had wanted to arrest him quietly because they feared the reaction of the crowd. Now they crept up on him in the dead of night. The disciples were asleep but Jesus was waiting up for them and offered no resistance. When Peter woke up, he sliced off the ear of one of the arresting party. Jesus reprimanded him. Peter was interfering with his strategy.

> *Put up thy sword into the sheath: the cup which my Father hath given me, shall I not drink it? (John 18:11)*

He was turned over to the High Priest Caiaphas and was tried and found guilty of blasphemy by claiming to be the Son of God. They in turn took him to Pontius Pilate, the Roman Governor, who proved reluctant to execute him and gave Jesus several opportunities to extricate himself but Jesus was not interested in release. Pilate, still unwilling to execute him, turned to the Jewish authorities and said: *I find in him no fault at all.* (John 18:38). But the Jews, probably whipped into a frenzy by the authorities, were baying for his blood. They screamed for Pilate to crucify him and unnerved him with claims that Jesus proclaimed himself King of the Jews. The threat to Pilate was clear. *If thou let this man go, thou art not Caesar's friend: whosoever maketh himself a king speaketh against Caesar.* (John 19:12).

Worried by the threat of incurring the wrath of the mighty Caesar, Pilate symbolically washed his hands of the affair, and agreed to have him crucified.

Public Execution

Jesus had to carry his cross through the streets of Jerusalem to a place called The Skull. It was a large spectacle as *there followed him a great company of people, and of women, which also bewailed and lamented him.* (Luke 23:27). Once he reached The Skull, he was nailed to the cross and hoisted high as an example to the on-looking crowd.

Mission Accomplished

According to John, Jesus' last words as he hung dying on the cross were: 'It is finished' (John 19:30). The words convey the meaning that the job was complete. Jesus had controlled events and implemented his four-point strategy – for him it was mission accomplished. By doing so, he launched a new religion and gave the world a new framework for life.

The Wisdom of Jesus

1. **Once embarked on a strategy, remain focused until the objective has been achieved.**
2. **Refuse to be deflected from reaching your goal.**
3. **Use conflict to raise awareness of the message.**
4. **Conduct conflict in public.**
5. **Be aggressive and forthright when confronting opposition.**
6. **Be prepared – anticipate the opposition's angles of attack.**
7. **Be prepared to get personal and raise the stakes in order to gain publicity.**
8. **Be prepared to make sacrifices in order to reach your goal.**
9. **Facilitate your opponent's plans if it assists your own objectives**
10. **Use big gestures to achieve impact.**
11. **Make the final act the climax of the strategy – aim to leave an indelible print on the audience's minds.**
12. **Set the final act into motion at the moment of maximum attention.**

6

Making Plans

Every business needs a clear objective and a clear plan of how to achieve that objective. A good plan is the route map to success, the way in which the objective is reached. A cohesive plan will focus the business, eliminate inefficiencies, harness resources, set deadlines and maximise human productivity.

We might be inclined to think that this level of planning is a modern day phenomenon - but we would be wrong. Jesus exhibited the same sophisticated planning techniques two thousand years ago. If we measure the success of the plan by the extent to which it achieved the set objective, then it was a flawless plan, perfectly executed. Jesus set out to ensure that *the gospel must first be published among all nations* (Mark 13:10) and he achieved it.

It is one of the striking features of Jesus' life that he bided his time for thirty years before he started his ministry and took centre stage (Luke 3:32). By waiting until he was thirty, Jesus not only gave himself time to grow *in wisdom and stature* (Luke 2:52) before he launched his crusade but he also allowed himself sufficient time to devise a winning plan.

Knowing the right time to launch a campaign is a key element in the appliance of any complex strategy. Over eagerness often forces the hand of less disciplined campaigners to start prematurely. Such impetuous upstarts are easily dealt with by experienced opponents who simply nip the 'problem' in the bud. Shrewd opportunists, such as Jesus, bide their time, waiting for the optimum moment to strike. In this aspect the waiting strategy is redolent of the skills required for the game of chess. An over zealous player in chess will rush for an early check-mate, sending all his forces down the board towards the opponent's King, creating gaping holes in his or her own defences. Such premature attacks are easily parried by experienced players who can consequently smash through their opponent's weakened guard. The world's greatest chess players bide their time, patiently building their forces by placing each piece in its optimum position. Only then do they strike. In chess, as in life, the effect is usually devastating.

Once Jesus did strike the momentum was relentless. From the moment that he met John the Baptist until his destiny with death, Jesus' ministry galloped along at breakneck speed. Conflicts, healings, rallies, public addresses, miracles, visits, story-telling, and conversions all happened at a startling pace. It is evidence of a man who knew exactly where he wanted to be and what he wanted to do. He had a master plan and he intended to see it through.

The scriptures reveal that Jesus was, by nature, a compulsive planner who devised plans to address all manner of situations from the minutiae of meal preparation to the determination of his own arrest and execution. In the same way that his father, Joseph, worked with wood to produce furniture, Jesus carefully honed and perfected his plans. For him planning was a way of life that enabled him to control events, influence outcomes and become the architect of his own destiny.

In essence plans provided the blueprint for his success. In this chapter we regard the design and careful construction of long, medium and short term plans as well as how he used research and time management to ensure that his plans actually succeeded.

Long-Term Planning

The recruitment of the disciples provides a good example of Jesus' long term clarity of purpose and forethought. The scriptures reveal a man who from the outset planned the use of human resources to achieve his ambitions. People had a major role to play in his communications strategy. He took time, therefore, to consider his options before starting his recruitment drive. Luke's and Mark's Gospels inform us that he recruited his disciples the morning after a night of contemplation. The next morning he went down to the shore of Galilee and targeted a particular type of person – he knew exactly who he was after. The scriptures state:

> *And Jesus, walking by the Sea of Galilee, saw two brethren, Simon called Peter, and Andrew his brother, casting a net into the sea: for they were fishers. (Matthew 4:18)*

At first it seems perplexing as to why he should attempt to recruit men busy at work. Why not approach some easier targets – say some men chatting on the shore? Or why not recruit more influential types, maybe religious leaders or those well versed in matters of doctrine? The targeting of labourers seems an oddity but the answer lies in the type of workers these were – for they were fishers. They were fishermen and fishermen have boats! He wanted to spread his message far and wide and boats were the fastest way of getting from A to B – especially around the Sea of Galilee where he started his ministry. With boats he had a battle bus – a campaign train. He could cover as much ground as possible in as little time as possible. Jesus chose his first disciples because they had transport!

> *And when he had gone a little farther thence, he saw James the son of Zebedee, and John his brother, who also were in the ship mending their nets and straightway he called them: and they left their father Zebedee in the ship with the hired servants, and went after him. (Mark 1:19-20)*

Again we see the same determination to secure boats. "When he had gone a little farther," he noticed men working in another boat "and straightway he called them" – Jesus purposefully targeted the boats.

It is significant that as soon as he had the boats, he started travelling around Galilee in earnest. Matthew says *he went about all Galilee, teaching in their synagogues, and preaching the gospel of the kingdom* (Matthew 4:23). Although boats are not specifically mentioned in this instance, we can have little doubt that boats were his preferred mode of travel. The use of boats are mentioned over forty times in the gospels. He put his campaign bus to good use.

Medium-Term Planning

Jesus needed human resources to execute his plans. As his ministry grew, he had to co-ordinate ever larger groups of dedicated helpers. This task required considerable forethought, planning and management. For Jesus, the question of help was one that he mulled over. He realised that there was huge potential for his message but became critically concerned about the lack of resources to convert all of the prospects.

> *Therefore said he unto them, "The harvest truly is great, but the labourers are few: pray ye therefore the Lord of the harvest, that he would send forth labourers into his harvest." (Luke 10:2)*

Jesus identified the issue of growing demand and limited supply before it became a major problem. Clearly Jesus did not anticipate this situation at the outset of his ministry but by addressing the issue early enough and by careful planning he was able to resolve it in the medium term. His solution was to recruit a further seventy followers who were permitted to preach on his behalf.

> ***Sea of Galilee***
>
> The early years of Jesus' ministry were spent largely in the region of Galilee especially the north-western shore of the Sea of Galilee, which dominated the region. The Sea of Galilee is in fact a large freshwater lake measuring 14 miles across at its widest point. It was the focus of a prosperous fishing industry as well as providing fertile terrain for agriculture. Whole communities depended on these two industries for their livelihood. Although an essentially Jewish region, it was proud of its distinctive culture and independence from the neighbouring region of Judea. Jesus grew up seventeen miles to the west of the southern tip of the Sea of Galilee in Nazareth which in those days was little more than a village. He later moved to the shores of the Sea of Galilee and took up residence in Capernaum, a large fishing town on the north-west shore of the lake. This was to be centre of his ministry.

Short-Term Planning

In the final days of Jesus' life, Peter and John asked Jesus what arrangements had been put in place for the Passover Meal. In typical fashion, everything had been organised. Jesus told them where to go, whom they should meet and how they would identify him. This individual in turn had been briefed to show them the room which had been reserved and had it fully prepared for the meal. There seems to have been a sense of wonderment at Jesus' organisational skills amongst the disciples as the scriptures make a point of stating that they everything was *found as he had said unto them* (Mark 14:16).

However, what the disciples were not aware of (but we now are) was that Jesus was just hours away from setting in motion his own arrest and execution. His ability, therefore, to remain composed and focused on small details, such as preparing a meal, was truly remarkable.

It was this eye for detail, coupled with his adeptness at seeing the big picture, that made him a uniquely influential person – one capable of controlling his own destiny, and ultimately that of the world too.

Intelligence Gathering

Good plans and decisions can only be made if the information they are based on is sound. Making grandiose plans without reference to the reality of the situation is futile. Modern day marketers spend huge sums on securing the best data, the latest information and most accurate research. A multi-million dollar research industry has grown out of the necessity for companies to garner accurate information on which to base their plans. Jesus understood the importance of accurate information too. He used his disciples for feedback so that he could plan his next moves.

> *And Jesus went out, and his disciples, into the towns of Caesarea Philippi: and by the way he asked his disciples, saying unto them, "Whom do men say that I am?" (Mark 8:27)*

In this case, Jesus wanted to know if his message was getting through. He needed to comprehend people's attitudes and so used his disciples as his eyes and ears. Through them he could canvass people's opinions and discern a more accurate picture of what was happening and how his message was faring. Jesus was canvassing people's opinions nearly two thousand years before the advent of market research.

Time Management

The gospels convey a sense of urgency. They give account of the relentless pace that Jesus set as he beat a trail around Galilee, Judaea and gentile (non-Jewish) territories. Indeed, Jesus' itinerary would have put even a modern day politician on an election campaign trail to shame.

Right from the start of his ministry, Jesus never eased up on the blistering pace he set from the start:

> *And straightway he called them: and they left their father Zebedee in*

> *the ship with the hired servants, and went after. And they went into Capernaum; and straightway on the sabbath day he entered into the synagogue, and taught. (Mark 1:20-21)*

The text reveals real urgency in Jesus' actions. He appreciated that time was a valuable commodity. Having devised a strategy which would deliver him success, he made sure that time was fully leveraged in order to deliver those plans. After he had finished in Capernaum, he disclosed his itinerary and informed that his disciples that they must keep moving:

> *And he said unto them, "Let us go into the next towns that I may preach there also: for therefore came I forth." And he preached in their synagogues throughout all Galilee, and cast out devils. (Mark 1:38-39)*

Eventually his fame was so great that the people followed him – even when he retreated into the desert. But rather than indulge his new followers, he told them that he could not stay with them – he had to move on to other cities, because that was his mission.

> *And when it was day, he departed and went into a desert place: and the people sought him, and came unto him, and stayed him that he should not depart from them. And he said unto them, "I must preach the kingdom of God to other cities also: for therefore am I sent." And he preached in the synagogues of Galilee. (Luke 4:42-44)*

Jesus was 'on tour'. He had a tight schedule and as much as he might have been tempted to take the soft option and stay with people who welcomed him, he kept on moving. He was driven by the necessity to spread his message and was tireless in his efforts to achieve it.

Throughout his ministry, he kept on the move by boat and on foot. He worked the Galilee region until he had sufficient critical mass to attract a crowd that would follow him to Jerusalem. Jesus was in many ways like an ancient election campaigner that had developed a hit-list of target areas then picked them off one by one.

In just three years, Jesus went from being a complete unknown to an omnipotent religious leader. He shook the authorities to their foundations; set Israel alight with his message; established a new doctrine; attracted thousands of followers and became a catalyst for world-wide change. Without planning and efficient time management, it is doubtful he could ever have achieved so much in so little time.

Synagogues

Synagogues became prevalent at the beginning of the Roman period. Their origins are not known but they are first mentioned in texts from about the first century AD. Each Jewish community had a synagogue (or assembly room) for the reading and analysis of scriptures, especially at the weekly meetings on the Sabbath. It functioned primarily as a venue for education rather than worship. Worship in synagogues became widespread only after the destruction of the Temple by the Romans in 70 AD.

The Wisdom of Jesus

1. **Take time to put plans together – avoid planning on the hoof.**

2. **Identify possible issues as early as possible.**

3. **Develop plans to resolve the issues before they turn into problems.**

4. **Use available resources to execute plans.**

5. **Build resources into your plans.**

6. **At the outset, ensure that you have sufficient resources to execute plans.**

7. **Once plans are formulated, don't be side tracked by soft options. Stay on track.**

8. **Use plans to prepare the smaller occasions in life as well as the large.**

9. **Have as much information as possible to help draw up plans.**

10. **Use time available as effectively as possible in the pursuit of objectives.**

PART 2

MARKETING, SALES AND COMMUNICATION TECHNIQUES

7

Building Awareness

The first principle of marketing is to make people aware of the product or service you are trying to sell. The reason is simple – people can not make a conscious decision to purchase a product if they are unaware of it. That is why marketers put huge amounts of effort, time and money into 'building awareness'.

In marketing, the ultimate aim is to achieve saturation awareness, i.e. everyone knows your brand. Some companies have come close to achieving this distinction: Coca-Cola, Marlboro, McDonald's and IBM are world famous, instantly recognisable brands. Christianity has achieved it too. But unlike the big brand names mentioned, its progress has not resulted from extensive advertising campaigns, complex promotional strategies or marketing think-tanks of a big budget corporation but rather on account of the zeal with which its apologists have preached its virtues down through the ages. The first proponent for Christianity was Jesus himself and all those 'preachers' who followed him have to some extent been inspired by him.

For Jesus, if there was a single objective he wanted to achieve above all others, it was to enable as many people as possible to hear about his ideology. Jesus believed that this was the very reason for his existence and his defining purpose in life. He was a man utterly focused on spreading 'the word' – it gave meaning to his existence. In characteristic fashion, Jesus was quite candid about the fact:

> *and he said unto them, "I must preach the kingdom of God to other cities also: for therefore am I sent." (Luke 4:42-44)*

and

> *And he said unto them, "Let us go into the next towns that I may preach there also: for therefore came I forth." (Mark 1:38)*

Ambition

Jesus was raised in an unremarkable town in rural Galilee and had limited experience of foreign nations outside the ancient region of Israel. That, however, did not diminish his ambitions – he wanted global awareness. He categorically stated his goal was for his message to be preached in all nations (Matthew 28:19). He fully acknowledged that it would not happen overnight – he saw it as a slow growing process which he likened to a seed growing into a tree. It was a superb comparison and also an accurate comparison. Christianity started from a single man trekking around towns and villages preaching his message of 'good news' to anyone who was to prepared to listen. From this humble start, Jesus set in motion the sequence of events which launched a way of life and a set of beliefs which have dominated the thinking and history of mankind for the last two millennia.

> *Then said he, "Unto what is the kingdom of God like? And whereunto shall I resemble it? Is like a grain of mustard seed, which a man took and cast into his garden; and it grew, and waxed a great tree; and the fowls of the air lodged in the branches of it." (Luke 13:18-19)*

Ancient Israel

The ancient land of Israel that Jesus lived in was dominated by the Mediterranean Sea along the Western shore and the River Jordan which ran parallel in a north-south direction, connecting the Sea of Galilee in the North and the Dead Sea in the South. The whole region was divided into several provinces recognised by the Romans: Idumea and Judea in the South; Samaria and Perea in the central region and Galilee and Decapolis surrounding the Sea of Galilee in the North. Each of the regions was ruled by one of Herod The Great's three sons Philip, Archelaus and Antipas, who was ruler of Galilee when Jesus was born.

Number Crunching

To achieve his global ambitions Jesus realised the need to preach his message to as many people as possible. He understood that he was playing a numbers game – the more people he preached to, the more converts he could win to his ideology. He illustrated the beautiful simplicity of the theory in the Parable of the Sower.

> *And he spake many things unto them in parables, saying, "Behold, a sower went forth to sow; and when he sowed, some seeds fell by the way side, and the fowls came and devoured them up: some fell upon stony places, where they had not much earth: and forthwith they sprung up, because they had no deepness of earth: and when the sun was up, they were scorched; and because they had no root, they withered away. And some fell among thorns; and the thorns sprung up, and choked them: but other fell into good ground, and brought forth fruit, some an hundredfold, some sixtyfold, some thirtyfold." (Matthew 13:3-8)*

The parable made a big impact on three of the gospel writers as it is covered in some depth in Matthew, Mark and Luke. Often the gospels do not explain the meaning of Jesus' sayings leaving the reader free to interpret them. As the meanings are not always transparent, some of them are the subject of heated debate. Fortunately, in the case of the Parable of the Sower, there is no doubt about its meaning as the gospel writers have recorded Jesus' explanation to his disciples. It is worth reading the full explanation

> *"When any one heareth the word of the kingdom, and understandeth it not, then cometh the wicked one, and catcheth away that which was sown in his heart. This is he which received seed by the way side. But he that received the seed into stony places, the same is he that heareth the word, and anon with joy receiveth it; yet hath he not root in himself, but dureth for awhile: for when tribulation or persecution ariseth because of the word by and by he is offended. He also that received seed among the thorns is he that heareth the word; and the care of this world, and the deceitfulness of riches, choke the word, and he becometh unfruitful. But he that received seed into the good ground is he that heareth the word, and understandeth it; which also beareth fruit, and bringeth forth, some an hundredfold, some sixty, some thirty." (Matthew 13:19-23)*

In this parable Jesus demonstrated his deep understanding of people and psychology. More importantly, he revealed the inner thinking of his own mind and in particular his attitude to marketing. It is patently clear that Jesus never expected or even intended to convert everyone to his cause. He acknowledged that rejection can happen for a host of different reasons and even categorised those who rejected his message into different genres.

The non-starters

The seed that falls by the wayside is the one that does not even take root. The prospects do not understand the proposition and so can not buy into it. The offer is too difficult or complex to comprehend and so is rejected without further consideration. The lack of response is almost as if the message had never been communicated at all.

The flash-in-the-pans

The seed which falls on stony ground is received with enthusiasm at first – but as soon the recipients come across some tribulation, objection or concern, doubts set in and they lose the will to embrace the proposition.

The Sybarites

The recipients of the seed thrown into thorns can not be bothered to buy into it if it is not convenient or easy. They are too busy chasing the easy delights of this world to concern themselves with a difficult proposition such as Jesus'.

The Good Prospects

Whatever the reasons for rejection, Jesus ultimately considered those genres to be an irrelevance – they were simply the responses he had to encounter in order to reach to the good prospects – those that repay him thirty, sixty and a hundredfold.

The one which falls on good ground repays the sower many times over – and makes up for all the rejections. This is the central tenet of selling. Put all the rejections behind you because as soon as you reach those that accept – their business can grow thirty, sixty or a hundredfold.

Putting Theory into Practice

The theory, therefore, is relatively simple: firstly, to maximise the numbers of good prospects it is necessary to communicate to as many people as possible; and, secondly, accept that rejection will happen as a matter of course.

He addressed the need to reach more people in three ways:

1. His first action at the outset of his ministry was to move to Capernaum, a more densely populated area than his home town of Nazareth. Capernaum was located on the north-west coast of the Sea of Galilee which was itself surrounded by other larger towns (Chorazin, Bethsaida, Magdala, Gennesaret). This area of Galilee was the region's centre of trade, culture and religion. It provided a fertile ground for Jesus' message and offered more potential converts than his home town.

   And leaving Nazareth, he came and dwelt in Capernaum, which is upon the sea coast, in the borders of Zabulon and Nephthalim. (Matthew 4:13)

2. Once there, his next task was to recruit helpers – the creation of a crack sales force formed a central plank in his marketing strategy. Jesus was realistic about the enormous task ahead. He knew it would take more than one man to spread his word to 'all the nations'. Helpers would be of critical importance. Indeed it was something that he fretted over. Without helpers to spread the word, Jesus realised that he might not achieve the critical mass that was required for his message to achieve wider acceptance.

   His band of loyal followers were trained by him to sell and disseminate his message. Again, it was a simple numbers game. The more people he recruited to actively propagate the message, the more widely known it would become. Jesus started with twelve helpers and later increased this number to seventy – a clear indication of the value he placed on effective sales people.

3. His third tactic was to go on the ancient equivalent of a whistle-stop tour. By covering as much ground as possible, Jesus could deliver his message to wider audiences. The gospels record that that he also travelled outside the Galilean region to Judaea, Decapolis, the cities of Tyre and Sidon, Jericho and ultimately Jerusalem. To cover this much terrain in three short years was a remarkable achievement. One of the ways in which he achieved

this was through the use of boats – the fastest mode of transport around the Sea of Galilee.

Jesus' travels

Jesus used Capernaum as his home base for his travels. From here he would embark on a series of lengthy expeditions, mainly throughout the Galilean region and in particular around the Sea of Galilee. He famously revisited his home town of Nazareth, situated in the centre of Galilee, and was hounded out by his own people. He also visited Cana where John reports that he converted water into wine. He is recorded as visiting many towns and villages including Bethsaida, Magdala and Gaderene. These towns were on opposite shores to each other and Jesus used boats to traverse the Sea of Galilee to reach them.

Both Matthew and Mark record that he journeyed as far North as the gentile town of Sidon in ancient Phoenicia which is located on the shores of the Mediterranean in modern day Lebanon. To the west, he travelled as far as a Roman port called Caesarea Philippi. Mark also reports that he travelled in the region of Decapolis (named after the number of cities in the region) to the east of Galilee, now modern day Syria and Jordan.

When he finally made his way to Jerusalem, he travelled down past the capital into Judea, probably passing through Samaria on the way. He then swept his way round the capital in a large arc and back up to Jericho – just ten miles to the East of Jerusalem. From there he travelled direct into the city, passing through the village of Bethany on the way.

The huge distances that Jesus covered is a measure of his immense drive and ambition. Especially when we consider that the vast majority of it was covered on foot.

Maintaining Momentum

The hectic schedule which he adhered to took discipline and dedication. In this respect he was a man with tunnel vision – all else paled into insignificance when compared with his need to communicate his message of salvation. Many times in the gospels there are occasions when Jesus was asked to stay by people who welcomed him – a tempting proposition for a tired man – but he refused to be blown off course and resolutely kept to his schedule (Luke 4:42-44).

Vantage Points – to be seen and heard

As the word of Jesus spread like wildfire the crowds that followed him grew bigger and bigger – *And the fame of him went out into every place of the country round about* (Luke 4:37). Huge throngs of followers would sometimes swamp him, even as he travelled between towns. On such occasions, Jesus was always sure to take the best vantage point for impact. On a famous occasion he preached from a mountain so that all the people would see and hear him – *And seeing the multitudes, he went up into a mountain* (Matthew 5:1). It was to be the setting for his Sermon on the Mount. On other occasions, when he was crushed on the shoreline he would take his boat out a little and preach from it. As ever, Jesus was always conscious of the need to find the best vantage point so that he was seen and heard by as many people as possible.

> *And he began again to teach by the sea side: and there was gathered unto him a great multitude, so that he entered into a ship and sat in the sea; and the whole multitude was by the sea on the land. (Mark 4:1)*

> *And he entered into one of the ships, which was Simon's and prayed him that he would thrust out a little from the land. And he sat down, and taught the people out of the ship. (Luke 5:3)*

When he was in towns and villages he nearly always made regular visits to the synagogues. Indeed, Mark tells us that he actually started his mission in a synagogue in Capernaum.

> *And they went into Capernaum; and straightway on the sabbath day he entered into the synagogue, and taught. (Mark 1:21)*

These places of worship were the centres of Jewish religious and cultural life and fertile ground for him to communicate his message – *and he taught in their synagogues, being glorified of all.* (Luke 4:15). Likewise, when in Jerusalem towards the end of his life, he arranged daily lectures in the Temple (even though he knew his life was in danger).

> *And all the people came early in the morning to him in the temple, for to hear him. (Luke 21:38)*

Wherever people were, there would Jesus also be.

The Wisdom of Jesus

1. **Make building awareness of your message a priority.**

2. **Set high awareness targets. People can only 'buy into' a proposition if they are aware of it.**

3. **Understand the reasons for rejection.**

4. **More importantly, however, accept that you must experience rejection in order to encounter good prospects.**

5. **Seek to reach the maximum number of people through whatever media channels are at your disposal.**

6. **Ensure you can meet demand for the message by recruiting other representatives who can communicate it too.**

7. **Generate as many opportunities to address audiences as possible.**

8. **Mount targeted campaigns to maximise the opportunities to sell.**

9. **When addressing an audience always ensure you procure the best vantage point.**

8

Public Relations

Any fool with deep pockets can advertise. Established media offer a plethora of communication channels on which to spend your money. Advertising space on TV, radio, newspapers, consumer magazines of every description, trade press, posters, cinema, milk bottle tops, petrol pump handles, and airships can all be bought. It is simply a question of how much.

The appeal of advertising is that it is 'safe'. Advertisers have the comfort of having complete control. They know when their campaign starts and finishes. They can regulate the extent of exposure, targeting it nationally or regionally, seeking broad audiences or niche markets. Moreover, advertisers can control the message, thereby eliminating the dangers of distortion and misinterpretation.

The Credibility Radar

Its strength, however, is also its Achilles heel. Consumers are ever more sensitive to the wiles of advertisers and readily discount advertising messages. Inured to a continuous stream of marketing messages, they see through the many intricately contrived ruses and, much to the frustration of advertisers, remain remarkably resilient to advertising campaigns. It is as if consumers have developed a 'Credibility Radar' through which the modern day consumer can detect and assess marketing messages in the blink of an eye. Like World War II bombers, many advertising messages are too easily caught by the radar and shot down in flames before the message has even reached the dropping zone. It is that brutal.

David Ogilvy, founder of advertising agency Ogilvy & Mather, famously stated in his book *Confessions of an Advertising Man* in 1963 that "half the money I spend on advertising is wasted and the trouble is I don't know which half." It is time to update Ogilvy's admission. In the nineties nearer two thirds is wasted – and rising.

Sneaking under the Radar

It is for this reason that marketing departments are putting increased emphasis on public relations. To advertise on a medium is one thing – but to persuade that same medium to endorse your product or service editorially is much more valuable. The message communicated is credible and slips effortlessly under the Credibility Radar, hitting the target. PR is the cruise missile of the marketing world.

It costs less too! Indeed it ostensibly costs nothing (although companies are increasingly relying on the services of PR Agencies that can charge a small fortune). Respectable media do not charge for editorial coverage. To charge would compromise their editorial freedom.

Superficially at least it seems to make sense to focus all marketing resources and energy into public relations – more credible, cheaper, better value. Unfortunately there is a downside. PR is a hazardous occupation. Firstly there is no guarantee of coverage, which risks breaking the first principle of marketing which is to build awareness. Secondly, if coverage *is* achieved, the communication can become distorted. Journalists add their own spin or interpretation to the original message. In the worst case scenarios, the media can play devil's advocate and champion the exact opposite of the view espoused in your original communication. To refine the earlier metaphor a little further, PR is like a Cruise Missile which is launched at a specific target but which sometimes gets its on-board computers jammed and starts to head back towards the launch pad!

The skill of the PR guru is to guarantee publicity and control the message – they keep the missile moving in the right direction.

On that definition, perhaps the person who most embodied the characteristics of a PR guru in modern times was Princess Diana. She was a world-wide media sensation, never out of the news. She was acutely aware of the voracious media appetite for her image and so was careful to stop and flash a smile. She also knew how to deliver a precise message. Her popularity never wavered even when she came to loggerheads with the powerful Royal Family. The image of her standing disconsolately in front of the Taj Mahal in India in the months before the break up of her marriage was, whatever else we may think of it, a virtuoso performance by the world's most photographed woman.

Jesus was a PR genius in a similar vein. He instinctively knew how to procure maximum publicity and how to control the message. Unlike Princess Diana, however, he operated in a virtual media vacuum. All he had at his disposal were two communication channels: those who were actually present when he spoke (which admittedly were often in their thousands) and the word of mouth network. Some thirty years after his death he had the assistance of the four gospel writers. His achievement in gaining so much notoriety given the lack of media is staggering and a testament to his genius.

A Copybook PR Campaign

Jesus' entry into Jerusalem was in essence a PR campaign – perhaps the most significant PR campaign of all time. Its impact on Jerusalem was of seismic proportions and the repercussions of it have spread like a tidal wave down through the centuries and are now rushing past us into future millennia.

Every stage was planned to communicate his message with maximum impact. He arrived on a donkey as prophesied in Zechariah, causing comparisons with the prophets. His followers spread garments in his way and cheered and welcomed him into Jerusalem like a triumphant king. The curious Jerusalem populace was informed by his followers that he was a prophet. The next day he strode into the Temple and ransacked the place. Capitalising on his notoriety, he proceeded to preach to the crowds daily. He also engaged in a series of confrontations with the authorities – all conducted in a very public forum. Finally, when his fame reached a new pinnacle, he pushed the authorities too far and effectively signed his own death warrant.

It was a mesmerising performance. All eyes were transfixed by him and his death was the PR coup of the millennium. By dying, he immortalised his message.

His behaviour may have been extreme but from a PR perspective it was a flawless, copybook campaign.

Creating a Stir

Jesus had shown himself to be a consummate practitioner of PR throughout his three years of preaching. John relates the story of another visit to Jerusalem which demonstrates an extraordinary PR instinct. The story starts as many people flock to the capital to celebrate the Festival of the Tabernacles. At this time, Jesus, fearing for his life, was trying to keep a low profile. His disciples, however, urged him to go along. Showing a basic grasp of PR themselves, they reminded their master that if he wanted a high profile then he could not act in secret.

> *His brethren therefore said unto him, "Depart hence, and go into Judaea, that thy disciples also may see the works that thou doest. For there is no man that doeth any thing in secret and he himself seeketh to be known openly. If thou do these things, show thyself to the world." (John 7:3-4)*

The incident confirms that Jesus did indeed "seeketh to be known openly" and, furthermore, demonstrated that the disciples had learnt the importance of public profile. Jesus' parables of the lamp hidden under a bushel[5] had not been in vain!

A Question of Timing

Jesus, however, had other motives for staying away other than his safety. He urged his disciples to go ahead as 'his time had not yet come.' Much is revealed by that single word 'yet'. He always intended to go – it was just a question of timing.

> *"Go ye up unto this feast: I go not up yet unto this feast: for my time is not yet full come." When he had said these words unto them, he abode still in Galilee (John 7:8-9)*

Then events took a curious turn. Jesus, far from keeping away from Jerusalem, did indeed go – but in secret. Unfortunately we do not know whether he went in disguise or whether he simply kept a low profile. Either way his efforts were totally effective. The public, unaware of his whereabouts, started to ask after him. Jesus, of course, was able to keep a close eye on developments and the crowd atmosphere as he was actually there.

> *But when his brethren were gone up, then went he also up unto the feast, not openly, but as it were in secret. Then the Jews sought him at the feast, and said, "Where is he?" (John 7:10 – 11)*

By his absence, Jesus became the hot topic for discussion. People became polarised in two opposite camps, some saying that he was a good man, others that he was a fraud. Controversy and intrigue surrounded him. Speculation and rumour were rife. By keeping away, Jesus had turned Jerusalem into a hotbed of gossip. His fame and notoriety were building by the hour.

> *And there was much murmuring among the people concerning him: for some said, "He is a good man: others said, Nay; but he deceiveth the people." (John 7:12)*

Jesus bided his time, waiting for the perfect opportunity to make a dramatic late entrance. Then, midway through the festival, just as most people would have given up on his attendance, Jesus made a theatrical appearance and immediately strode up to the Temple to teach. Jesus had centre stage and the spotlight was on him.

> *Now about the midst of the feast Jesus went up into the temple, and taught (John 7:14)*

Like a great singer who saves the best song until last, Jesus made his best and most memorable speech on the last day of the festival.

> *In the last day, that great day of the feast, Jesus stood and cried, saying, "If any man thirst, let him come unto me, and drink. He that believeth on me, as the scripture hath said, out of his belly shall flow rivers of living water." (John 7:37-38)*

Jesus showed star quality. He sparked controversy, courted conflict and was the biggest topic of conversation. He had maintained his position at the top of the bill. From a PR perspective, it was a dream campaign, a sparkling performance.

The whole episode reaffirms the sharp mind and shrewd instincts of Jesus. He showed perfect timing, a keen eye for the big opportunity and a profound understanding of human behaviour. By studying Jesus' marketing motivations we can see design in everything that Jesus did and said.

The Reverse PR Technique

As well as possessing a complete grasp of strategy, Jesus was a master PR tactician capable of using specific techniques to engineer the desired effect. One tactic which served him particularly well appears on the surface to contradict his sworn mission to spread his message. As a result of its contradictory nature, I have called it Jesus' 'Reverse PR Technique'.

There were many occasions when Jesus seemed to seek unnecessary secrecy over his actions. He frequently instructed individuals not to discuss their encounters with him – particularly if he had performed an amazing act. Some examples follow:

- After curing a man with leprosy, he said: *"See thou tell no man"* (Matthew 8:4).
- After curing a little girl who was thought to be dead, he instructed the parents that *no man should know it.* (Mark 5:43).
- After curing a deaf and dumb man, he charged them that they should tell no one (Mark 7:36).
- On another occasion, he cured a blind man and said *"Neither go into the town, nor tell it to any in the town."* (Mark 8:26)

The Reverse PR Technique Explained

On each occasion Jesus appeared quite firm that he did not want these individuals to disclose the details of his wondrous deeds. This of course goes against the grain of human nature. If we witness an astonishing feat, we find it practically impossible to contain our enthusiasm – we simply have to tell someone. Scratch away at the surface of these stories, however, and we realise that Jesus was playing psychological games and never seriously expected the events to be kept secret.

In the first case of the man cured of leprosy, Matthew reports that large crowds witnessed the event (Matthew 8:1). Telling the leper to be discreet is one thing but expecting a large crowd to keep a secret – totally impossible. The leper of course could not stop himself either. He *went out, and began to publish it much, and to blaze abroad the matter, in so much that Jesus could no more openly enter into the city, but was without in desert places: and they came to him from every quarter.* (Mark 1:45). Some secret!

Turning to the case with the little girl – again Jesus had a large group of people in attendance. They were wailing because they thought the girl was dead. When Jesus stated that she was really only sleeping they laughed at him. Jesus then told the girl to get up, which she duly did. Incredulity turned to astonishment. He must have known that instructing the parents to keep silent about the apparent saving of their daughter was a human impossibility. And quite pointless too when there was a tribe of awe-struck eye witnesses present.

Healing a deaf and dumb man and then asking him not tell anyone is patently amusing. You have to wonder whether, through the centuries, we can see a mischievous sense of humour – asking a cured mute not to speak to anyone as to how he was now speaking!

The act was once again conducted in front of a group of people who were *beyond measure astonished, saying, "He hath done all things well: he maketh both the deaf to hear, and the dumb to speak."* (Mark 7:37)

The blind man too was cured in front of an audience. Discretion was impossible. Jesus knew full well that secrecy from individuals who had witnessed something extraordinary was highly improbable. Obtaining collective secrecy, as they were always conducted in public, was impossible. The reason he performed the Reverse PR Technique is actually explained in the gospels. After he cured the deaf and dumb man, Mark made this observation:

And he charged them that they should tell no man: but the more he charged them, so much the more a great deal they published it. (Mark 7:36)

Jesus once again showed he was a master of psychology. He knew that adding an element of secrecy actually made it all the more exciting! It made the wondrous events even more intriguing and mysterious. As Mark says – the more he told them not to – the more they did.

There can of course be no doubt that his demands for people to keep these events secret were hopelessly ineffective – we still discuss them two thousand years later.

Damage Limitation

As already mentioned, PR is a hazardous business and, like many practitioners of PR, Jesus had his difficult moments too. He once made a disastrous trip to Gaderene. He arrived, disembarked from his boat, exorcised a devil and was promptly blamed for sending a herd of pigs off a cliff. The destruction of a whole herd undoubtedly had a big impact on many people's livelihoods who were dependent on rearing farm animals. The dismay the event caused in the community is transparent and understandable:

> *Then the whole multitude of the country of the Gadarenes round about besought him to depart from them; for they were taken with great fear: and he went up into the ship, and returned back again. (Luke 8:38)*

They wanted him to go and quickly. Jesus' response was exemplary – he did exactly what he was asked. He made no attempt to defend his actions; he did not offer explanations; he did not apologise. He just left.

Many accident prone politicians could learn from Jesus' approach. How many times have we witnessed politicians sink deeper and deeper in a quagmire of accusations by standing there and defending the indefensible to the hilt? If you are in a hole, stop digging.

Conflict and Controversy

On other occasions, however, Jesus used conflict to his advantage. It is well documented that Jesus was engaged in a running battle with the authorities and in particular with the Pharisees. One factor common to all of the clashes is that each and every one of them was conducted in public – often in front of large crowds. There is no evidence in the gospels that Jesus tried to settle his differences with them privately. He relished the conflict. Confident in his ability to outwit them, he knew that conflict brought drama, notoriety and afforded him favourable comparisons with the unpopular authorities. Jesus had no interest in resolving the conflict. For him it was a highly effective PR tactic. News of his skirmishes would travel countrywide, bringing more and more people into contact with Jesus and his message.

The Wisdom of Jesus

1. **Use PR to sneak under the 'Credibility Radar'.**

2. **Schedule PR campaigns to coincide with major events.**

3. **Use the late arrival technique to start tongues wagging.**

4. **Typically arrive just as people are giving up hope of your arrival.**

5. **Save your finest stunt, speech or address until last.**

6. **Use the Reverse PR Technique if you achieve a major success. Asking people to keep quiet surrounds the event in mystique and fuels excitement even more.**

7. **In the case of an embarrassing or disastrous PR situation, simply walk away. When in a hole, stop digging. Under all circumstances avoid defending the indefensible.**

8. **Use controversy and conflict to the good of your cause. Build public interest and fuel discussion by conducting skirmishes in public.**

9

Endorsement

Modern day marketers recognise the importance of third party endorsement. Considerable budgets are spent on procuring PR agencies which can manipulate the media to make favourable comment about a company, product or service. Sceptical consumers are more inclined to react favourably to a proposition if it comes from an independent source. Some industries, such as film and the theatre, are crucially dependent on favourable media coverage. No amount of advertising can resurrect the reputation of a production which has been savaged by the critics.

Marketers also seek another kind of endorsement – that of the celebrity. The concept is simple enough. Marketers seek to associate their product or service with a well known and admired star. It might be that they are fabulous looking movie stars, extraordinarily gifted sports stars, extremely funny comedians or in-vogue pop icons. If they are seen to be drinking brand x and wearing brand y, there are thousands of fans who will aspire to emulate them – such is the power of association.

Nike has built a sportswear clothes empire on this strategy. The founder of the company, Phil Knight, started the business in his father-in-law's basement in 1964, selling most of his shoes to high school athletics teams. Knight fully appreciated the power of endorsement and his shoes were seen for the first time in serious competition at the 1972 Olympic trials. In 1973 Nike paid world class runner and controversial figure Steve Prefontaine to wear Nike shoes. It was the start of a concerted effort to recruit the best and most renowned athletes in the world to wear Nike gear. Indeed, the sports stars which were recruited to endorse Nike read like a sporting Hall of Fame: Carl Lewis in athletics; John McEnroe and Andre Agassi in tennis; Bo Jackson in baseball (and American Football); Michael Jordan in basketball; and Renaldo and the Brazilian team in football. In 1996 he signed Tiger Woods, a 20 year old golfer for $40 million. In 1997 Woods won the US Masters by a record margin and Nike sales in golf merchandise grew by 100%. In the same year Nike had a turnover of $9 billion, with profits of $795 million, and was established as one of the world's top ten brands. Meanwhile Phil Knight, who started out as a student runner, became one of the three richest men in America. Endorsement works!

Jesus understood the power of endorsement too. There are numerous examples of him actively seeking it. In ancient Israel there was no film, sport or pop industry. The only type of person which generated fanatical followings were religious 'celebrities'. Right at the start of his ministry Jesus sought the endorsement of a major religious luminary called John the Baptist.

John the Baptist had his own distinct set of disciples and a large following. Mark states that *there went out unto him (John the Baptist) all the land of Judaea, and they of Jerusalem, and were all baptised of him in the river of Jordan, confessing their sins* (Mark1:5). To have the endorsement of this man would have been the best possible start to Jesus' own ministry. The gospels state that before he started his ministry, even before he recruited his disciples, he went to John to be baptised. John duly did so and of Jesus he proclaimed:

> *"There cometh one mightier than I after me, the latchet of whose shoes I am not worthy to stoop down and unloose. I indeed have baptised you with water: but he shall baptise you with the Holy Ghost." (Mark 1:7-8)*

John the Baptist

John the 'Baptiser' (Mark 1:4) advocated baptism for the forgiveness of sins – a rite which involved cleansing through the submersion and washing of people in a river or stream. The gospel writers all describe him identically as – *The voice of one crying in the wilderness, "Prepare ye the way of the Lord, make his paths straight."* (See Matthew 3:3, Mark 1:3 and Luke 3:4). They echo the prophet Isaiah who foretold of a forerunner to the Messiah that *crieth in the wilderness, "Prepare ye the way of the Lord, make straight in the desert a highway for our God."* (Isaiah 40:3). He lived an austere life, wore camel's skin, and fed on locusts and wild honey – a lifestyle which identifies him with the prophet Elijah.

John was later arrested and imprisoned by King Herod the Tetrarch, the ruler of Galilee, and ultimately beheaded on his instruction. However, Herod had been reluctant to execute John as he *feared John, knowing that he was a just man and an holy* (John 6:20). He was, however, tricked into executing him after he promised Salome, his wife's daughter, anything she wanted, after she performed a dance on his birthday. After consultation with her mother, who had a grudge against John because he had denounced her marriage to Herod as unlawful[6], she demanded the head of John. Herod reluctantly acceded to her demand.

When Herod first heard of Jesus, he feared that it was John the Baptist risen from the dead.

John the Baptist professed that he was not fit to undo the thongs of his sandals! This was endorsement indeed.

John's gospel gives more detail of the encounter. When the Baptist saw Jesus he announced:

> *"Behold the Lamb of God, which taketh away the sin of the world. This is he of whom I said, 'After me cometh a man which is preferred before me: for he was before me. And I knew him not.'" (John 1:29-31)*

Moreover he went on to say:

"but he that sent me to baptise with water, the same said unto me, 'Upon whom thou shalt see the Spirit descending, and remaining on him, the same is he which baptiseth with the Holy Ghost.' And I saw, and bare record that this is the Son of God." (John 1:31-34)

Jesus had a ringing endorsement from one of the most famous preachers in Judaea. This proclamation along with the ritual baptism marked the coming of age for the carpenter's son. He was ready to begin.

The Value of Endorsement

The value of John's endorsement to Jesus cannot be underestimated. It was Jesus who stated that for him to make great claims about himself was of no value – but because John the Baptist had made great claims on his behalf, then it was verifiable truth!

"If I bear witness of myself, my witness is not true. There is another that beareth witness of me; and I know that the witness which he witnesseth of me is true. Ye sent unto John, and he bare witness unto the truth. But I receive not testimony from man: but these things I say, that ye might be saved." (John 5:31-35)

The Upward Prestige Spiral

The value of endorsement is only as good as the reputation and standing of the endorser. To be endorsed by an unpopular liar and cheat is worthless and probably counter-productive. Jesus was careful, therefore, to enhance the good name of John the Baptist:

"Verily I say unto you, Among them that are born of women there hath not risen a greater than John the Baptist" (Matthew 11:11)

When he spoke of why people went to see John the Baptist he stated:

"But what went ye out for to see? A prophet? Yea, I say unto you, and much more than a prophet." (Luke 7:26)

By mutually endorsing each other, Jesus and John created an upward prestige spiral, each benefiting from the other's support.

Inclusive Strategy

Jesus was not, however, just looking for 'celebrity' endorsement; he welcomed it from every quarter. When his disciples informed Jesus that they had prohibited a man from casting out devils in his name, Jesus reprimanded them:

And John answered him, saying, "Master, we saw one casting out devils in thy name, and he followeth not us: and we forbad him, because he followeth not us." But Jesus said, "Forbid him not: for there is no man which shall do a miracle in my name, that can lightly speak evil of me. For he that is not against us is on our part." (Mark 9:38-40)

Jesus demonstrated an inclusive approach to the communication of his message. He was not insistent that only 'authorised' personnel could spread the Good News. This inclusive strategy is one of the great strengths of Christianity. Any Christian can, and is actively encouraged to spread his message – as opposed to restricting its marketing to, say, just the clergy. Therefore Jesus created a sales force of thousands. Today it is counted in its millions.

Outposts

Jesus sometimes used those who would endorse him strategically to represent him in areas and regions that he had insufficient resources to maintain a presence in. At the Gaderene debacle, when he was held responsible for destroying a herd of pigs, there was one man from the region who still held Jesus in high esteem – the man he cured of possession by demons! This man 'begged' Jesus to permit him to follow him – but Jesus refused. Jesus had another plan for him:

> *And when he was come into the ship, he that had been possessed with the devil prayed him that he might be with him. How be it Jesus suffered him not, but saith unto him, "Go home to thy friends, and tell them how great things the Lord hath done for thee, and hath had compassion on thee." (Mark 5:18-19)*

Through this man's endorsement, Jesus maintained a presence in a community which had no reason to be fond of him. The tactic proved very effective:

> *And he departed, and began to publish in Decapolis how great things Jesus had done for him: and all men did marvel. (Mark 5:20)*

The Wisdom of Jesus

1. **Use 'celebrity' endorsement to create credibility.**

2. **Obtain endorsement before a campaign is embarked on. People tend to give more credence to your message if it already has the endorsement of an independent and respected third party.**

3. **Seek the most ringing endorsement possible. People will scrutinise the claims of a third party.**

4. **Return the compliment to your endorser and build his or her reputation. Mutual endorsement builds an Upward Credibility Spiral.**

5. **Consider those that are not against you to be for you. If individuals or organisations espouse the benefits of your company, product or service, don't gag them. Let them endorse you.**

6. **Seek to have endorsement in areas or markets where you have poor sales, image or representation. Strategic endorsement is a powerful technique for acquiring market penetration.**

10

The Mind Medium

The average person is hit by hundreds of commercial messages everyday. In the morning we switch on the radio and hear six or seven commercial messages in every advertising break; we stroll down to breakfast and read the special promotion on the back of a cereal packet; on the way to work we buy a newspaper which consists of over 30% advertising; stuck in a traffic jam we notice the strategically placed posters; when we arrive at work subliminal messages are sent by a gamut of branded items on our desk (calendars, diaries pens, etc.); if we surf the net, nearly every page of millions is selling a concept of some kind; when we return home in the evening we slump in front of the television for an intensive diet of advertising. Such is life today. In Jesus' time, however, there was no comparable media infrastructure and yet his message spread like a ripple in a pond across the world.

The Mind Medium

Jesus' technique was to use the medium in people's minds – their imagination! Everyone can see events unfold through their mind's eye

– they just need to be told what to watch.

Consider this – most of the readers of this book can close their eyes and see the Prodigal Son approaching his father's home to be welcomed as a long lost son. Likewise many of us can see the Good Samaritan helping the man beaten by brigands by the roadside. In fact these events never happened – they were told by a storyteller two thousand years ago.

So many of Jesus' messages are wrapped in stories and comparisons called parables. He used them as the primary way of addressing and educating the crowds that followed him. Matthew states that *he taught them many things by parables* (13:3) and Mark reports that he spoke to them exclusively in parables – *but without a parable spake he not to them* (4:34).

Parables

The word parable comes from the Greek 'parabole' which essentially means comparison. There are eighty stories in the gospels which can be described as parables. Jesus often used scenes from everyday life in his parables. In particular he drew parallels with fishing and agriculture which would have been very familiar to Galileans – many of whom who were farmers or fishermen.

The importance of the technique to Jesus is clear. He believed that this was the best and most appropriate way to teach. By using parables he could package complex messages in an exciting and easy to understand format and challenge the listener to find the inner meaning. With his disciples, however, he never risked misinterpretation and frequently took them aside to explain in full the meaning hidden within.

The power of parables is illustrated by the story of the Good Samaritan. Jesus was asked by an expert in law *"And who is my neighbour?"* (Luke 10:29). It pays to read Jesus' full reply:

The Good Samaritan

> *And Jesus answering said, "A certain man went down from Jerusalem to Jericho, and fell among thieves, which stripped him of his raiment, and wounded him, and departed, leaving him half dead. And by chance there came down a certain priest that way: and when he saw him, he passed by on the other side. And likewise a Levite, when he was at the place, came and looked on him, and passed by on the other side. But a certain Samaritan, as he journeyed, came where he was: and when he saw him, he had compassion on him, and went to him, and bound up his wounds, pouring in oil and wine, and set him on his own beast, and brought him to an inn, and took care of him. And on the morrow when he departed, he took out two pence, and gave them to the host, and said unto him, 'Take care of him; and whatsoever thou spendest more, when I come again, I will repay thee.' Which now of these three, thinkest thou, was neighbour unto him that fell among the thieves?" And he said, "He that showed mercy on him." Then said Jesus unto him, "Go, and do thou likewise." (Luke 10:30-37)*

This story has everything. A man travelling alone from Jerusalem to Jericho; robbers and a violent beating; men of good standing in the community who refused to help; and a Samaritan, despised by the Jews, who nursed the hapless traveller back to health. What a compelling answer and how much more riveting than the simple prosaic answer the story contains – that everyone is your neighbour.

Samaritans

The Samaritans are a tribe that broke away from mainstream Judaism about 400 BC. They are a conservative group which maintains that the Torah (the first five books of scriptures) is sacred but reject all subsequent oral and scriptural law. Because of their break from Judaism, the tribe was despised by the Jews. Indeed, for the last two thousand years, the Samaritans have been persecuted by the Romans, Jews, Christians and Muslims. Today there are only about 600 Samaritans left.

The technique is effective and has stood the test of time – the fact that we can still recount these stories today is proof enough of that.

Jesus used two types of parables. Some contained an underlying message as in the case of the parable of the Good Samaritan. He used others to make short, straight forward comparisons such as the parable of the Pearl:

> *Again, the kingdom of heaven is like unto a merchant man, seeking goodly pearls: Who, when he had found one pearl of great price, went and sold all that he had, and bought it. (Matthew 13:45-46)*

By using parables Jesus met several of his objectives:

- Parables are an effective way of communicating complex moral issues. Fairy tales and myths passed from generation to generation work along the same principle.
- Parables also work well as an eloquent way of making simple comparisons.
- Parables can make a message more relevant.
- Parables have a greater impact on the listener.
- Parables are easy to remember and are easily recounted.

It is worth studying the technique in more detail. Selected parables are outlined in the following information box.

The Main Parables

Parable	Comment	Text
Lamp under a bowl	Jesus espouses the importance of spreading the message	Matthew 5:14-15, Mark 4:21-22, Luke 8:16, 11:33
House on a rock	The importance of following Jesus' principles	Matthew 7:24-27, Luke 6: 47-49
The sower	The selling of the message, rejection and rewards	Matthew 13:3-8, 18-23, Mark 4:3-8, 14-20, Luke 8:5-8, 11-15
Weeds	The separation of people into 'good' and 'bad' at the end of time	Matthew 13:24-30, 36-43
Mustard seed	The growth of the Kingdom of God from very small beginnings	Matthew 13:31-32, Mark 4:30-32, Luke 13:18-19
Valuable pearl	The value of attaining the kingdom of heaven	Matthew 13:45-46
Net	The sorting of good and bad people at the end of time	Matthew 13:47-50
Lost sheep	The importance of each convert to God	Matthew 28:12-24, Luke 15:47
The unforgiving servant	The importance of forgiving others	Matthew 18:23-24
Workers in the vineyard	God even accepts latecomers into the Kingdom of Heaven	Matthew 20:1-16
The wedding feast	Only a few make it into heaven	Matthew: 22:2-14
Ten virgins	Be prepared for the coming of God	Matthew 25:1-13
Talents	The importance of investing one's talents	Matthew 25:14-30
Sheep and goats	Treating others with compassion	Matthew 25:31-46
Watchful servants	Keep alert for the coming of God	Mark 13:35-37, Luke 12:35-40
Good Samaritan	Everyone is a neighbour	Luke 10:30-37
Friend at midnight	Be bold and ask	Luke 11:5-8
Rich fool	The emptiness of material gain	Luke 12:16-21
Cost of discipleship	The burden of following Jesus	Luke 14:28-33
Lost coin	The importance of each convert	Luke 15:8-10

The Wisdom of Jesus

1. **Use the screen in people's minds to project your message – harness the power of imagination.**

2. **Communicate complex messages through metaphors which contain the meaning within. Challenge the listener to find the inner meaning.**

3. **Use imagery which is relevant to the people you are targeting.**

4. **Use parables for greater impact. Even prosaic truths can become interesting when communicated through a metaphor.**

5. **Use parables so people can more easily recall and recount your message.**

6. **To avoid misinterpretation, ensure that your team are aware of the meaning of the metaphors.**

11

The Art of Selling

The importance that Jesus placed on selling can not be overstated. According to Matthew, the very last words Jesus spoke to his disciples were his command to go out to the whole world, spread his message and win converts. Whether they were actually his last words is largely irrelevant. The gospel writer knew it was of such huge importance to Jesus that it warrants being placed as Jesus' final command.

> *And Jesus came and spake unto them, saying, "All power is given unto me in heaven and in earth. Go ye therefore, and teach all nations, baptizing them in the name of the Father, and of the Son, and of the Holy Ghost: teaching them to observe all things whatsoever I have commanded you: and, lo, I am with you alway, even unto the end of the world. Amen." (Matthew 28:18-20)*

Star Salesman

Jesus himself was an extraordinarily good sales person. His rate of conversion of people to his cause was phenomenal. What made his persuasive powers all the more remarkable was that he was asking people to change their way of life. Today's marketers spend enormous energy and money convincing purchasers to switch from one brand to another – be it a car, bar of soap, toothpaste or beer. This may be very important in a marketing context but it is hugely unimportant in the big scheme of things. Jesus, on the other hand, was asking people to make changes which were demanding, inconvenient and fundamental. Indeed, he asked people to put others before themselves and to make personal sacrifices. And yet millions upon millions of people have responded to his message. This chapter analyses seven of the sales techniques that helped make him such a supremely effective and successful sales person.

1. Getting Noticed

There is a modern expression that sums up Jesus' approach to sales better than any other and it is 'in your face'. If someone is 'in your face' you can not ignore them, you can not avoid seeing them, you have to take notice. Jesus wanted his followers to behave in much the same way. He told them that they should shout the message from the rooftops.

> *"What I tell you in darkness, that speak ye in light: and what ye hear in the ear, that preach ye upon the housetops." (Matthew 10:27)*

For Jesus, there was no question of being meek and timid. He believed that if you have something worthwhile to say you should make it heard.

> *"No man, when he hath lighted a candle, putteth it in a secret place, neither under a bushel[4], but on a candlestick, that they which come in may see the light." (Luke 11:33)*

and

"Ye are the light of the world. A city that is set on an hill cannot be hid. Neither do men light a candle, and put it under a bushel, but on a candlestick; and it giveth light unto all that are in the house. Let your light so shine before men, that they may see your good works, and glorify your Father which is in heaven." (Matthew 5:14-16)

Jesus makes the promotion of his message a central tenet of being one of his followers. He expects them to be the *"light of the world"* that *"will shine before men"*. The first principle of selling, therefore, is to be brash, bold and up front i.e. get noticed.

2. Persistence

Jesus believed in asking once, asking twice and then asking again. He believed it to be an imperative to keep asking. Every time that a sales person asks for business is an attempt to close the sale. Ask, ask and then ask again and it will be given to you.

"Ask, and it shall be given you; seek, and ye shall find; knock, and it shall be opened unto you: for every one that asketh receiveth; and he that seeketh findeth; and to him that knocketh it shall be opened." (Matthew 7:7)

Children have mastered this particular technique. Have you ever been with a child which keeps asking for something that has caught his or her eye, a sweet perhaps or a toy. They ask the question once, twice and many, many more times – can I have that? And how many times have we witnessed parents caving in just to find some peace. As adults, we tend to forget this devastatingly effective technique but Jesus never did. He told this parable to teach the principle:

Saying, "There was in a city a judge, which feared not God, neither regarded man: and there was a widow in that city; and she came unto him, saying, 'Avenge me of mine adversary.' And he would not for a while: but afterward he said within himself, 'Though I fear not God, nor regard man; yet because this widow troubleth me, I will avenge her, lest by her continual coming she weary me.'" And the Lord said, "Hear what the unjust judge saith." (Luke 18:2-6)

3. Courage

As well as being persistent, Jesus told his disciples to be bold when asking. Ask for whatever you want, whenever you want. If it is an awkward time – ask anyway. Jesus believed that the more of an irritant you are – the more likely the prospect will capitulate to your demand – just to get rid of you!

And he said unto them, "Which of you shall have a friend, and shall go unto him at midnight, and say unto him, 'Friend, lend me three loaves; for a friend of mine in his journey is come to me, and I have nothing to set before him?' I say unto you, Though he will not rise and give him, because he is his friend, yet because of his importunity he will rise and give him as many as he needeth" (Luke 11:5-8)

4. Knocking Copy

In his usual frank style, Jesus had no scruples about 'going negative' on opponents' messages. In particular he warned of the philosophies of the Pharisees and Sadducees.

Then understood they how that he bade them not beware of the leaven of bread, but of the doctrine of the Pharisees and of the Sadducees. (Matthew 16:12)

It is common practice in modern day marketing to avoid talking down a rival's product or service. Sales people are often exhorted to 'rise above' such practices. Some marketers are concerned that a confrontational approach can lead to a mudslinging match. This is possibly true but if you are the only one not throwing mud – you are the only one with mud on your face.

Jesus showed no such scruples. If he detected a flaw or defect in his opponents' positions or arguments he was prepared to point it out publicly. From a personal perspective I have always recognised knocking copy as a powerful marketing technique.

Some years ago, I set about buying a new car from one of two manufacturers. The first manufacturer conducted a completely professional sales pitch. When I told them I was also considering buying a car from a rival manufacturer they told that it was a good brand too. No mudslinging – totally professional. However, when I visited the rival showroom and informed the salesman that I had test driven another car he immediately responded: "Good cars but did you hear about their gear box problems?" When I replied that I was unaware he went on to tell me that they had to order a whole batch of them back to be refitted as "apparently there had been a few nasty accidents".

It was a great hatchet job on the opposition. As safety was a decisive factor in my purchasing decision, I naturally bought the second car.

5. Black and White Alternatives

Jesus gave his audiences stark alternatives – sweet repose for those that followed him and damnation for those that did not. He frightened errant followers while making loyal followers feel exceedingly special. His skill was to contrast the huge benefits of heeding his message with the black consequences of ignoring it. It meant that not only were people drawn to his doctrines because of the positive aspects – they were also scared of the downside. By painting black or white extremes, Jesus left no room for ambivalence. People given black or white options are forced to think seriously of their position.

The White

In Matthew's Gospel, Jesus assured his audience that those that follow him have life's burdens lifted and will be given rest (Matthew 11:28-30). What music to the ears of the down-trodden and weary.

Jesus immediately went on to contrast this idyllic picture with infernal scenes saved for those who reject his message. The hellish picture he depicted served as a startling wake-up call for anyone thinking that opting out is an acceptable alternative.

The Black

Then began he to upbraid the cities wherein most of his mighty works were done, because they repented not: "Woe unto thee, Chorazin! Woe unto thee, Bethsaida! For if the mighty works, which were done in you, had been done in Tyre and Sidon, they would have repented long ago in sackcloth and ashes. But I say unto you, It shall be more tolerable for Tyre and Sidon at the day of judgment, than for you. And thou, Capernaum, which art exalted unto heaven shalt be brought down to hell: for if the mighty works, which have been done in thee, had been done in Sodom[7], it would have remained until this day. But I say unto you, that it shall be more tolerable for the land of Sodom in the day of judgment, than for thee." (Matthew 11:20-24)

The use of scare tactics are an underrated and underused selling tool. Modern day marketers tend to concentrate almost exclusively on communicating benefits. Jesus, on the other hand, used benefits and the downside of rejection in a powerful selling mix.

Down through the ages, the fire and brimstone element of Jesus' approach has been adopted by many preachers who 'put the fear of God' into people. Unfortunately, they tended to focus exclusively on the dark side, thereby terrifying people into obedience. In the long term, however, this can be counter-productive. An audience driven solely by fear often rebels.

The technique works best when it is mixed with the benefits as

Jesus did. The audience then at least can embrace the proposition for positive reasons. The technique certainly works – many thousands of devout Christians have led good and honourable lives out of love and fear of God in equal measures.

6. Hospitality

Tired and hungry people are in no position to buy a complex proposition. They can not concentrate on the intricacies of the offer until they have been rested and fed. Apart from the humanitarian aspects of feeding people, Jesus understood that the base needs of people must be addressed before they can be sold to. There were two very famous occasions when Jesus organised the feeding of thousands of people.

> *And they that did eat were four thousand men, beside women and children. (Matthew 15:38)*

Sales people are advised to provide nourishment and refreshments for their prospects. Tea, coffee, biscuits and sandwiches are a welcome sight for any hungry person. Once sated, the prospect is able to concentrate better on the sales pitch.

7. Leave them wanting more

There were numerous occasions when Jesus refused invitations to remain with people who had invited him to stay longer. Jesus never outstayed his welcome with any hosts and like a good politician knew the pitfalls of over-familiarity. (As we will see in the next chapter, he learnt this lesson the hard way when he suffered outright rejection by his home town of Nazareth.) Excessive exposure can lead to a loss of respect. Jesus was a leader and leaders can undermine their own position by being excessively available. It can damage a leader's image and by association the message that they espouse. Jesus understood when it was time to move on and that was as soon as the job was done.

And when it was day, he departed and went into a desert place: and the people sought him, and came unto him, and stayed him that he should not depart from them and he said unto them, "I must preach the kingdom of God to other cities also: for therefore am I sent" and he preached in the synagogues of Galilee. (Luke 4:42-44)

The Wisdom of Jesus

1. **Make sure you get noticed – be brash, be bold, be up front.**

2. **Consider your sales pitch as a service. Buyers want to know what you have to say.**

3. **Ask, ask and then ask again. Persistence pays off.**

4. **Have courage when asking. Be prepared to ask even when it is inconvenient or inappropriate. Prospects will often accede to your demands to get rid of you!**

5. **Be prepared to knock the flaws in a competitor's proposition. Going negative works.**

6. **Paint a black and white picture contrasting the advantages of accepting the proposition with the disadvantages of rejecting it. Ensure that indifference is not an option.**

7. **Only give the downside alongside the upside for your proposition.**

8. **Look after your prospects' welfare. Ensure they are well fed, healthy and relaxed before attempting to sell.**

9. **Avoid over familiarity with prospects.**

10. **Know when to stop. Once you have sold, stop and move on to the next target.**

12

Handling Rejection

Jesus believed that the single biggest asset in successful sales people was their ability to handle rejection. He saw rejection as a pernicious force undermining sales people. Knock-backs sap sales people's self-esteem and their belief in their own proposition. The corollary is a lack of confidence which in turn leads to unconvincing sales pitches, further rejection and so on. A lack of belief in the ability to sell becomes a self-fulfilling prophecy and successful conversions to business dive into a steep tailspin. Some sales people will recognise the symptoms described. Many sales jobs have an incredibly high turnover of staff because employees can not stomach the constant rejection. Part of the problem is that people take it personally – they feel a rejection of their proposition is a rejection of them too. It hurts to feel rejected and Jesus experienced more than his fair share.

Bitter Experiences

On returning to his hometown, Jesus suffered complete rejection. The people that Jesus grew up with could not accept his new elevated status. They saw him as acting above his station and refuted his lofty claims and new reputation. To them he was still the carpenter's son from down the road – certainly not as a prophet or the Messiah.

> *And he went out from thence, and came into his own country; and his disciples follow him. And when the sabbath day was come, he began to teach in the synagogue: and many hearing him were astonished, saying, "From whence hath this man these things? And what wisdom is this which is given unto him, that even such mighty works are wrought by his hands? Is not this the carpenter, the son of Mary, the brother of James, and Joses, and of Juda, and Simon? And are not his sisters here with us?" And they were offended at him. But Jesus said unto them, "A prophet is not without honour but in his own country, and among his own kin, and in his own house." (Mark 6:1-6)*

Luke gives us even more detail of the incident and shows that the situation turned distinctly nasty:

> *And all they in the synagogue, when they heard these things, were filled with wrath, and rose up, and thrust him out of the city, and led him unto the brow of the hill whereon their city was built, that they might cast him down headlong. (Luke 4:28-29)*

His home town was so incensed by Jesus that they were intent on killing or maiming him. Fortunately for him, he made a lucky escape. He had not sustained physical injury but their reaction must have hurt him in other ways. The people whom he had known from his childhood and early adult years gave him no chance. They would not listen to what he had to say because of their familiarity with him. They could not accept that this man from humble beginnings could hold a world changing vision for the future.

Jesus had experienced rejection – an important occurrence in his life and the way he handled it formed the basis for tackling all future rejections. He simply walked away – he did not retaliate or resist – he just moved on, agreed to disagree and sought his next target.

> *But he passing through the midst of them went his way, and came*

down to Capernaum, a city of Galilee, and taught them on the sabbath days. (Luke 4:30-31)

Nazareth

Nazareth is commonly accepted as the childhood home of Jesus although there is some confusion as to when his family first moved there. Luke maintains that Mary and Joseph moved there before the birth of Jesus while Matthew states that they moved there after a period in exile in Egypt. Most historians accept that his formative years were spent there. The town is situated approximately 20 kms away from the Sea of Galilee to which Jesus would move at the start of his ministry. Matthew, Mark and Luke all record how Jesus was treated with disbelief in the Synagogue there – all the more poignant as this was his home town.

There were other occasions when Jesus was made unwelcome such as when he was held responsible for destroying a whole herd of pigs in the region of Gaderene (believed to be on the East coast of the Sea of Galilee).

On arrival there, a man possessed by demons ranted and raved at Jesus. Jesus reportedly cast the devils out of the man and into nearby swine. The swine promptly ran over a cliff and were destroyed. Although Jesus is blamed for the incident, there is the prosaic possibility that the demonically possessed man startled the pigs and caused a stampede.

Whatever the true cause of the mayhem, the pig handlers ran into the town, recounted the incident and placed the blame on Jesus. The town was quite naturally incandescent. A stranger and his followers had come into their region and through the use of special powers committed a herd of valuable pigs to their death. Not unsurprisingly they remonstrated with him and implored him to leave the region.

And, behold, the whole city came out to meet Jesus: and when they saw him, they besought him that he would depart out of their coasts. (Matthew 8:34)

Jesus could have quite justifiably defended his position, but instead set a shining example for his disciples on how to handle this rejection. He just upped and went – no remonstrations, no prevaricating, no defensive remarks – he just dusted himself down and went home.

And he entered into a ship, and passed over, and came into his own city. (Matthew 9:1)

As usual, the disciples were slow to learn. On another occasion when he was made unwelcome by the Samaritans on his way to Jerusalem, the disciples urged Jesus to send down fire from heaven to consume them (Luke 9:54). Jesus was apoplectic with their attitude. Despite everything that Jesus had said and done, they still did not understand the manner in which he wanted rejection handled. They wanted revenge but Jesus told them that there would be no retribution and simply moved on to the next village. Jesus' response, in stark contrast to his disciples, was calm and composed. He was not one to let rejection stop his progress or divert him from his cause.

Being Realistic

Empirically, Jesus knew the hazards of rejection – it had been an all too familiar experience in his own life. He knew that to play down its impact was unrealistic and ultimately counter-productive. Jesus was, therefore, quite open and frank about the level of rejection his disciples might face. The Parable of the Sower is all about the rejections that must be encountered before fertile prospects, which make it all worth while, are reached. Indeed, Jesus prepared them for the worst and warned some of them that they might even be slain for the cause! (Matthew 10:28) He did not believe in pulling his punches. He knew that by preparing his disciples for extreme eventualities, they were better equipped to deal with difficult situations as and when they actually occurred.

In the course of events, some disciples did, as predicted, meet their deaths as a result of their proselytising. The heroic way in which they handled their violent ends has been the cause of much admiration for Christians and non-Christians alike down through the centuries. Undoubtedly it was Jesus who gave them the strength to face such adversity.

Protection from Rejection

Although, Jesus regarded rejection for a sales person as a simple fact of life, he did not believe in being exposed to its damaging impact if it was possible to avoid it. He made a special effort to insulate his disciples from rejection – especially in their formative training years. When Jesus sent them on a mission to spread his message he instructed them to work in pairs and to avoid the 'city of the Samaritans'. He was acutely aware that they would need the moral support of colleagues and that the cold reception they would have received from the Samaritans was an experience that could smash their fragile confidence. Preaching to the Jews was problem enough at that stage.

Dealing with Rejection

Complete protection from rejection, however, is impossible. In reality, many people would make them unwelcome. In these circumstances, Jesus set down a simple procedure he wanted his disciples to follow.

> *"And if the house be worthy, let your peace come upon it: but if it be not worthy, let your peace return to you. And whosoever shall not receive you, nor hear your words, when ye depart out of that house or city, shake off the dust of your feet." (Matthew 10:13-14)*

Jesus gave them a two point plan to follow:

1. He told them to accept rejection with equanimity. He urged them to let 'your peace return to you' and not to be ruffled or upset. In modern day parlance we would say 'don't let it get to you' – just accept it and move on.

2. He asked them to shake the dust off their feet and depart. It is a psychological gesture as much as anything – a ritual which helps to put the issue behind you and erase the incident from the mind. By dusting yourself down, you distance yourself from the affair, cease all further involvement and move on – the best possible reaction to a negative experience.

The Wisdom of Jesus

1. **Jesus encouraged his disciples to understand that rejection is not a failure, just a fact of life. It happens and there is little that can be done about it. In his Parable of the Sower, Jesus described the sorts of people who rejected the proposition and the reasons why. In the search for fertile prospects, some of your sales pitches will inevitably fall on deaf ears.**

2. **Acknowledge the worst possible scenarios – prepare for the worst.**

3. **Do not expose yourself or your staff to unnecessarily high levels of rejection – go for softer targets first.**

4. **As rejection is just a fact of life like the rising of the sun, it is important to not take it to heart. It happens to everyone. It certainly happened to Jesus.**

5. **When rejection is encountered, simply dust yourself down and move on to the next prospect – that next one might be a good prospect and 'yield a hundredfold' thus making up for all previous disappointments.**

13

Image, Style and Content

Speaking with Power

Throughout the New Testament there are references to crowds being 'astonished' by Jesus. People were drawn to him wherever he went – even out in the desert. We can deduce from the reaction of the crowds that Jesus was a virtuoso performer.

> *And they were astonished at his doctrine: for his word was with power. (Luke 4:32)*

He had a style and charisma which captivated audiences. Enthralled, they would hang on to his every word. Such was his power that even hardened soldiers, sent to capture Jesus, forgot their duty and fell under the spell of his oratory powers.

> *And some of them would have taken him; but no man laid hands on him. Then came the officers to the chief priests and Pharisees; and they said unto them, "Why have ye not brought him?" The officers answered, "Never man spake like this man." (John 7:44-46)*

This was not the only occasion when he was saved by his ability to command the attention of a crowd. In Jerusalem the authorities were thwarted daily because of the spellbound reaction of the throng.

> *And he taught daily in the temple. But the chief priests and the scribes and the chief of the people sought to destroy him, and could not find what they might do: for all the people were very attentive to hear him. (Luke 19:47-48)*

Earlier in his ministry it was his oratory powers confounded and alarmed his own countrymen.

> *And all bare him witness, and wondered at the gracious words which proceeded out of his mouth. And they said, "Is not this Joseph's son?" (Luke 4:22)*

As we have noted, on this occasion the townsfolk were impressed to the point where they became incredulous. The locals could not believe their own eyes and ears. It was easier to reject him outright than acknowledge that one of their own could rise to be a sensation.

Alas, we will never know some aspects of his style such as how he dressed, the timbre of his voice, the passion of his delivery and how he gesticulated. What a huge privilege his followers had to witness this world-changing man in action. Jesus was indeed right when he said privately to his disciples, *"Blessed are the eyes which see the things that ye"* (Luke 10:23)

However, we can glean from the scriptures something of his style and approach. We can study the content, packaging and oratory techniques used by Jesus in his speeches and with a little imagination almost see the brilliant orator in full flow as he worked the crowds. Moreover we can then apply the same techniques for a more successful style of communication in our own careers.

Languages

Galilee stood on the cross roads of many high traffic trade routes from the surrounding regions. As such it attracted a cosmopolitan crowd and many languages were spoken. It is quite possible that Jesus was multilingual. He would certainly have spoken Aramaic, the native language of Galilee, and Hebrew, a closely related language which was widely used in religious situations. He would also have been familiar with Greek, which was spoken by travellers from the neighbouring region of Decapolis. Latin was frequently spoken too, particularly by the ruling Roman occupiers. He would have come across this language more frequently in Jerusalem and the Roman port of Caesarea Philippi.

Talking with Authority

A frequent theme of the scriptures was that Jesus spoke with authority and power. Jesus earned the right to be considered an authority because of his superb knowledge of the scriptures, theology and doctrine. By demonstrating deep knowledge and expertise he was elevated to the status of expert. He was someone whose views mattered and were much sought after.

His total grasp of the subject matter meant that he often outshone his opponents - who themselves claimed to be experts but often fell short of being so. Even the crowds themselves could discern the greater 'authority' of Jesus.

> *And they were astonished at his doctrine: for he taught them as one that had authority, and not as the scribes. (Mark 1:22)*

The Source of Authority

For the Jewish race the scriptures represent the word of God spoken through prophets and so provide the basis for all beliefs, practices and law. The messages and views expressed in the scriptures are considered to be those of God himself and were, therefore, right and true. Nearly all matters, right down to tiny details of washing and eating habits, were determined by what the scriptures said on the matter.

Jesus held the scriptures in the highest regard. For him it was a sacred text which contained the immutable facts of life. He considered the scriptures the ultimate sanction of the arguments he developed and, therefore, took great care to ensure that his position was fully backed by them. To attempt to change the words of God by even the smallest amount was for him the most heinous crime imaginable.

Evolution not Revolution

Jesus, therefore, carefully avoided undermining the scriptures, defining the new doctrine that he championed as the fulfilment of scriptures not as a radical alternative. Politically Jesus positioned himself as a moderniser who brought legitimate and timely change. His circumspect approach avoided the alienation of many devout Jews who, like people the world over, welcome change but not through extremism or the through the complete obliteration of all the main principles on which they based their lives.

In the UK, Prime Minister Tony Blair achieved a similar feat with the Labour Party. He campaigned for the amendment of a restrictive clause in the party's constitution called Clause 4 which tied the party to the nationalisation of industries and the redistribution of wealth. After eighteen years in opposition, Blair wanted to make the Labour Party 'fit for Government' and electable in the eyes of the public. Amending Clause 4 had a deep symbolic significance and was a part of the process of change. He was wily enough, however, to pitch his changes as part of a program of 'modernisation'. He did not talk of scrapping the old standards and tenets but of building on them. The

Labour Party backed him and together they went on to win the 1997 election with a record landslide victory.

'Evolution not revolution' is an important principle to grasp. It enables those who seek change to seize the 'centre ground' and avoid being pushed to the outer edge where they can only exert marginal influence on people's lives. Jesus by contrast managed to develop extraordinary popular appeal and ultimately influenced the lives of billions of people. He achieved this by building on people's beliefs not by destroying them.

> *"Think not that I am come to destroy the law, or the prophets: I am not come to destroy, but to fulfil. For verily I say unto you, till heaven and earth pass, one jot or one tittle shall in no wise pass from the law, till all be fulfilled." (Matthew 5:17-18)*

Power of Knowledge

His expertise in doctrine was the result of many hours of study and an unquenchable thirst for knowledge. From an early age he immersed himself in his religion, learning and debating with the most learned men. There is the story in Luke's gospel of Jesus at the age of twelve going to Jerusalem with his parents for the Passover festival. On leaving Jerusalem, Jesus slipped away from his parents and stayed behind in Jerusalem. The parents did not in fact find him for three days but when they did, *they found him in the temple, sitting in the midst of the doctors, both hearing them, and asking them questions.* (Luke 2:46)

The occasion shows a rebellious streak in the young boy. But more than that it highlights his thirst for knowledge. Even at an early age he showed prodigious talent for learning and debating the scriptures.

> *And all that heard him were astonished at his understanding and answers. (Luke 2:47)*

Later the young boy returned to his home town of Nazareth and continued to grow *in wisdom and stature, and in favour with God and man.* (Luke 2:52)

Manifesto

It was in those formative years and early adulthood that Jesus developed his own philosophy for life. By debating with learned men and accumulating knowledge Jesus honed and perfected his belief system. By the time he was thirty he was ready to unveil it and did so in dramatic fashion when he addressed thousands of followers out in the desert at the start of his ministry.

It is no coincidence that this address was the first major speech of his ministry. This was Jesus' pledge to the people - his manifesto.

> *"Blessed are the poor in spirit: for theirs is the kingdom of heaven. Blessed are they that mourn: for they shall be comforted. Blessed are the meek: for they shall inherit the earth. Blessed are they which do hunger and thirst after righteousness: for they shall be filled. Blessed are the merciful: for they shall obtain mercy. Blessed are the pure in heart: for they shall see God. Blessed are the peacemakers: for they shall be called the children of God. Blessed are they which are persecuted for righteousness' sake: for theirs is the kingdom of heaven. Blessed are ye, when men shall revile you, and persecute you, and shall say all manner of evil against you falsely, for my sake. Rejoice, and be exceeding glad: for great is your reward in heaven: for so persecuted they the prophets which were before you." (Matthew 5:3-5:12)*

This address holds enormous religious and historical significance. It represents Jesus' first major departure from Judaism. Jesus was in fact establishing a new creed. Christians refer to the occasion as the Sermon on the Mount or the Beatitudes. It is commonly believed that it took place on the eponymous Mount of Beatitudes which is situated close to Capernaum. The hill overlooks the tranquil blue waters of the Sea of Galilee and blue tinged hills beyond. The effect is serene and uplifting - the perfect backdrop for Jesus' message of hope.

From an oratory viewpoint and from an historical perspective this was one of the greatest addresses of all time. It had an electrifying effect on his audience who were 'astonished' at his teaching (Matthew 7:28). Moreover, it has since formed the backbone of many modern day political movements and is still interpreted and preached from Christian pulpits world-wide. Its impact is undeniable and anyone interested in the business of communication can do no better than to learn lessons contained within this inspirational maiden speech.

Sound Bites for Impact

In the address Jesus uttered a series of short, succinct sayings. This style enabled him to inculcate his message into the audience. They in turn could more easily memorise and reiterate it. In Jesus' day this oral tradition was well established - people would pass on important information by continual reiteration. The trick is to make it memorable.

It is ironic that this ancient technique should make a big comeback in the twentieth century with the advent of television. High profile politicians and media celebrities are encouraged to make short dramatic 'sound bites' which can fit into a brief TV news broadcast. PR gurus know that TV may allocate just five or six seconds for a quote - there is no place for a lengthy statement. Even complex issues must condense down to pithy sayings.

Making it Relevant

Another technique he employed to stunning effect was to make it relevant to his audience. They were poor, down-trodden, hungry, thirsty and unappreciated. Politically they were an oppressed people burdened with crippling taxes from Rome. Jesus understood their plight, he recognised their hardship and used it to reach them. He systematically identified their worries, grievances and concerns and gave each of them cause for comfort. His message of hope found a willing and receptive audience. The result of his brilliant speech was not unexpected. *When he came down from the mountain, great multitudes followed him.* (Matthew 8:1)

The skill of making his communication relevant to his target audience was a technique that he employed to good effect throughout his ministry. People identified with his speeches because he empathised with them. He showed he understood their concerns, fears, needs and aspirations. His speeches came alive because he addressed people in a personal manner.

Some of the very first words that Jesus is credited with in Mark's Gospel are a lesson in making a message relevant. It was the occasion when he strolled along the shores of Galilee looking to recruit some fishermen to his cause. His opening gambit was not to construct a logical argument as to why they should follow him but to give them a dynamic concept that they could immediately relate to. This approach encapsulated the message he wanted to communicate in a germane and intriguing way - he told them he wanted them to be *"fishers of men"*. The approach was original, totally relevant and worked. Peter, James and John became his closest friends and confidants. Together they went on to change the world.

> *And he saith unto them, "Follow me, and I will make you fishers of men." (Matthew 4:19)*

The Feel Good Factor

There is no doubt that in the Sermon on the Mount Jesus made his audiences feel better about themselves. Whatever their plight he gave reason for comfort. It was an approach that he would use throughout his ministry. Consider the comfort he must given to people who were poor, hungry and lacking in decent clothes with the following address:

> *Therefore take no thought, saying, What shall we eat? Or, What shall*

we drink? Or, Wherewithal shall we be clothed? (For after all these things do the Gentiles seek:) for your heavenly Father knoweth that ye have need of all these things. But seek ye first the kingdom of God, and his righteousness; and all these things shall be added unto you. Take therefore no thought for the morrow: for the morrow shall take thought for the things of itself. Sufficient unto the day is the evil thereof. (Matthew 6:31-34)

Jesus was saying, don't worry about food, drink or clothing! Seek God and all these things will be given to you. Don't worry about tomorrow either - let tomorrow take care of itself. There is enough to worry about today.

What soothing notions for the afflicted! Is it any wonder he won followers?

Polemical Skills

Jesus was not always engaged in speeches to receptive audiences. There were also those who aimed to destroy him and this required a quite different approach.

To combat them he depended on his wits, his supreme grasp of the scriptures and a solid education. The education that Jesus procured gave him invaluable knowledge and insight into his own religion and culture. It provided him with an overview of the society in which he lived and it was from this position that he could develop his world changing doctrines. It was the foundation for his philosophy and the launch pad for his New Kingdom. It enabled him to put forward powerful arguments extolling the virtues of the message or to construct water-tight defences when under attack.

Jesus superior knowledge and polemical skills enabled him to engage with opposing sects and win the doctrinal debate. Many times he used his command of the scriptures to score points and undermine his opponents. He often left them floundering in his wake, unable to counter his hard hitting verbal volleys. An attempt by the Sadducees to trip him up with an arcane question was typical. They asked who a woman would be married to after she died if she had married seven times during her life. Jesus was able to answer the question using the scriptures to support his argument. He also took the opportunity to taunt them for their lack of knowledge

> *"Ye do err, not knowing the scriptures, nor the power of God." (Matthew 22:29)*

It was a recurring theme of Jesus' tempestuous relationship with the authorities. Many times he embarrassed his opponents by pointing out their inadequate knowledge of the scriptures:

> *And he answered and said unto them, "Have ye not read that he which made them at the beginning made them male and female." (Matthew 19:4)*

At other times he more than embarrassed them - he used the scriptures to humiliate them and even sully their 'good' name. The approach was brutally effective:

> *And he taught, saying unto them, "Is it not written, 'My house shall be called of all nations the house of prayer?'[8] But ye have made it a 'den of thieves'[9]." (Mark 11:17)*

Aggressive Defence

His exceptional grasp of the scriptures and law enabled him to think on his feet and turn the tables on opponents. He often dealt with aggressive inquisitors by moving onto the offensive, directing well-aimed scriptural observations at the heart of their argument. Foes capitulated under the weight of his onslaught.

> *Then the Pharisees and scribes asked him, "Why walk not thy disciples according to the tradition of the elders, but eat bread with*

unwashen hands?" He answered and said unto them, "Well hath Esaias prophesied of you hypocrites, as it is written, 'This people honoureth me with their lips, but their heart is far from me. How be it in vain do they worship me, teaching for doctrines the commandments of men.' [10] *For laying aside the commandment of God, ye hold the tradition of men, as the washing of pots and cups: and many other such like things ye do." (Mark 7:5-8)*

Jesus used the scriptures to highlight their own hypocrisy and foil their devious attempts to snare him.

Preparation

Jesus was so quick to use the scriptures in his defence, it is probable that he anticipated the Pharisees' line of attack and prepared his responses in advance. When they criticised him for allowing his disciples to pick ears of corn on the Sabbath (as this was considered work), Jesus quoted three different scriptural sources to scupper their attack.

But he said unto them, "Have ye not read what David did, when he was an hungred, and they that were with him; how he entered into the house of God, and did eat the show bread, which was not lawful for him to eat, neither for them which were with him, but only for the priests? Or have ye not read in the law, how that on the sabbath days the priests in the temple profane the sabbath, and are blameless? But I say unto you, that in this place is one greater than the temple. But if ye had known what this meaneth, 'I will have mercy, and not sacrifice"[11]*, ye would not have condemned the guiltless. For the Son of man is Lord even of the sabbath day." (Matthew 12:2-9)*

Real Reflections

Jesus used communication to deal with the authorities and court the people. He did it with style and élan and on his own. He did not have a PR agency, spin doctor, speech-writer or image consultant. Neither did he have the privilege of vetoing bad copy after an interview or the option to 'take two' for recorded television. In some ways Jesus lived in a more real world than our own. There was no opportunity to artificially enhance his image. What you saw is what you got - which makes his impact all the more impressive.

The Wisdom of Jesus

1. **Ensure that you have a deep and sound knowledge of your subject matter - become an authority.**

2. **Build on people's belief systems - evolution not revolution. This approach avoids the alienation of your audience and enables you to grab the centre ground.**

3. **Offer change but not extremism.**

4. **Make an effort to become fully educated in your chosen area of expertise.**

5. **Realise that knowledge is power.**

6. **Create sound bites which are succinct, easy to memorise and encapsulate a message.**

7. **For maximum impact when addressing an audience, make it relevant to them.**

8. **Identify with your audience - make them feel welcome and important.**

9. **Address and empathise with the concerns, fears, needs and aspirations of your audience.**

10. **Only engage in a debate on a subject of great import when you have expert knowledge of the topic.**

11. **Make sure you are better versed than your competitors.**

12. **Use your expert knowledge to expose the flaws in your opponents' argument or position.**

13. **Anticipate and prepare for encounters with audiences, media or competitors.**

PART 3

SALES TEAMS, TRAINING AND MOTIVATION

14

Creating a Sales Machine

Organising Manpower

Lao Tze, the ancient Chinese philosopher and founder of Taoism, stated that *a journey of a thousand miles must begin with a single step*. Six hundred years later the founder of Christianity made his first step by striding down to the harbour in Capernaum and seeking the help of others. He was under no illusion about the scale of the task ahead. The launch of a new world doctrine required planning, effort and resource. Recruiting followers into his organisation was a top priority – he knew he could not market his vision without human resources.

Jesus was deliberate and systematic about the formation of his organisation. Empirical evidence suggests that he had a clear structure in mind that he pieced together bit by bit. Each piece played a critical role in the selling and distribution of his message. Taken as a whole Jesus founded one of the most effective, dynamic, and enduring sales machines of all time.

The organisation consisted of a five-tiered, pyramidal hierarchy. Jesus himself was placed at the top with layers of command and responsibility below him.

Tiered Pyramidal Hierarchy

Level	Tier	No.
1	Jesus as master and leader	1
2	An inner team of close confidants	3
3	The lead sales team	12
4	Approved sales force	70
5	All other followers	Thousands

Jesus was extraordinarily good at attracting followers. In ancient Israel, he was the equivalent of a modern day superstar with thousands of people flocking to him. People travelled huge distances to see him or just to touch the hem of his robe in the belief that he could cure them. From the many thousands that followed him he selected just twelve to be his lieutenants. They were called his disciples or apostles. The word apostle comes from the Greek *apostolos* which literally means "one who is sent out", a term that closely relates to the modern term 'agent' – one who has full authority to represent the one who sent them. Later, as demands on him grew, he expanded the number of followers that could represent him to seventy. Throughout it all, he maintained an inner sanctum of three followers who were also his closest friends – Peter, James and John.

Tier 1 – Master and Leader

Jesus was at the apex of the pyramid. Like a feudal lord he was the undisputed master and leader. On no occasion was he reported to have consulted his disciples. On no occasion did he seek their opinion. His organisation was autocratic and, in characteristic fashion, he was quite candid about the fact:

> *"The disciple is not above his master, nor the servant above his lord." (Matthew 10:24)*

By his own admission, Jesus viewed his disciples in the same way a lord sees his servants. Given the time period, this placed the disciples in a lowly position indeed. By this definition, Jesus was essentially all-powerful while his disciples held only basic rights.

Jesus did not, however, abuse his position of authority. On the contrary, Jesus was a hard but fair master. He showed great concern for their welfare, he led by example, and he trained them extensively. To him they were always more than a group of hangers-on or lackeys – they were of crucial importance. He needed them to fulfil a vital role in his marketing strategy.

Tier 2 – The Inner Team

Jesus selected three men, Peter and the brothers James and John to form an inner team of close confidants that was treated with special favour. On the famous occasion when he was said to have cured a little girl who had allegedly died (but whom he said was simply asleep), Luke states that he did not let anyone into her room except for Peter, James, John and the parents. At the time, Jesus was undoubtedly surrounded by hysterical, wailing and confused people and his gut instinct was to banish them all save for the mother, father and those he trusted. The story infers a special relationship between Jesus and Peter, James and John. That intimation is fully corroborated by other incidents.

Three of the gospels[12] relate an occasion of great Christian significance called the Transfiguration when Jesus led the three up a mountain and exclusively revealed his divinity to them. Christians and atheists will argue long and hard as to what exactly did really happen – but whatever it was, it had a major impact and the gospel writers pay particular attention to the fact that Jesus chose to share this moment exclusively with Peter, James and John.

Perhaps most significantly, at the time of Jesus' greatest anxiety, as he waited in the Garden of Gethsemane for the authorities to arrest him, it was with Peter, James and John that he wished to spend his last moments alive. The Gospel of Mark relates how he became deeply distressed and troubled and was moved to exclaim to them:

> *"My soul is exceeding sorrowful unto death: tarry ye here, and watch." (Mark 14:33-34)*

At the moment of critical distress and deep personal crisis he wanted his close colleagues there for support. He tellingly did not ask for the support of any other of his disciples who were all nearby.

To some degree, this is a story we can all relate to. None of us has experienced the harrowing wait for executioners to arrive but we have all had times of anxiety, fear or depression. At those precise moments, we reach out for certain individuals for moral support. In the clearest way possible, the story shows that Peter, James and John were more than just 'servants' to a cause, they were his dearest friends.

Heirs Apparent

Jesus' overriding ambition, however, was to spread his message. Jesus knew that he would be leaving his disciples and that he needed a group to lead his followers after his demise. Jesus set about grooming the inner team as potential leaders. After his death, Peter and John did in fact become the leaders of the early Church guiding it through the first treacherous years. James was executed early on by King HerodKing Herod.

The temperament of the individuals whom Jesus allowed to draw close to him is of great significance as it is those individuals who helped to build the early Church after his death. We are fortunate that of all the disciples, most is written about these three (Peter in particular features prominently). The scriptures thus enable us to appreciate their traits, tendencies and characteristics.

Fellow Countrymen

We are not entirely sure where most of the disciples originated from. It is postulated that Philip, for instance, came from a Greek city in the Decapolis region – but we can be sure. In contrast, we know for certain that the first four disciples, Peter, Andrew, James and John lived on the banks of the Sea of Galilee 'for they were fishermen'. Jesus was raised just a day's walk away from the Sea of Galilee in Nazareth. He was familiar with the people and the region which prided itself on its distinctive culture and separateness from Judaea and Jerusalem. These were people he had grown up with, understood and felt comfortable with – a good starting point for a lasting relationship.

However, It took more than just being a Galilean to be one of Jesus' confidants. Andrew who was called to be a disciple on the same day as Peter, James and John, never made it into the inner team. More was required. Jesus wanted:

- Passion
- Loyalty
- Leadership
- Passion

Passion

Peter was a fiery character. He was quarrelsome, outspoken and susceptible to violent mood-swings. He frequently stepped out of line, earning brutal admonishments from Jesus. But Peter meant well. His ebullience and over-zealous nature were the result of a fierce devotion to Jesus. On the two occasions he received his most serious reprimands from Jesus, it was because he was anguished by the prospect of Jesus' death and was desperate to prevent it. In some respects they were endearing qualities which Jesus made allowances for and even admired.

Less is written about James and John but with his nickname for the brothers being 'Sons of Thunder', they could hardly have been the shy and retiring type! The name suggests that they were loud, boisterous even mercurial. Like Peter they showed a bellicose streak. When Jesus was made unwelcome by a Samaritan town, James and John urged Jesus to raze the city to the ground with fire!

Their passion for the fight stood them in good stead after Jesus' death. They encountered many confrontations with the authorities yet remained outspoken and resolute apologists for their beliefs. This bravery and dogged persistence were the same qualities that had epitomised their master before.

Loyalty

Loyalty was the quality that Jesus looked for in all of his followers. The loyalty of his inner team was intense. Peter made big sacrifices to follow Jesus. The scriptures infer that he left his wife, home, family and business (Luke 18:28-30). Indeed Peter once boasted that he would be prepared to die for him (John 13:37). He was as good as his word and sacrificed his life for the cause in Rome some years later. James followed a similar path. It was the unwavering loyalty of these men that helped turn Christianity into a phenomenon.

Leadership

All three demonstrated leadership qualities. Peter was effectively the unofficial spokesperson of the twelve disciples. When tax collectors approached the disciples to determine whether Jesus was paying taxes, it was Peter whom they quizzed. It was Peter who often stepped forward to ask Jesus to explain a parable. It was Peter who took the initiative and was first to tell Jesus that he believed him to be the Messiah (Mark 8:29). Peter was effectively second in command.

James and John were keen to have their places reserved in the pecking order too. They brazenly asked Jesus to guarantee their position as his second-in-commands (Mark 10:37). When the other disciples heard of their effrontery, they reacted with hurt indignation. Jesus, wary of a possible split amongst his disciples, had to gather the whole band together swiftly for a pep talk in order to heal the rift.

Jesus had seen enough, however, for him to nominate Peter as his leader designate. Peter had the right mix of qualities. After Peter had proclaimed him as the Messiah, Jesus appointed Peter as his heir: *"thou art Peter, and upon this rock I will build my church; and the gates of hell shall not prevail against it."* (Matthew 16:18).

Tier 3 – The Lead Sales Team

Peter, James and John were actually part of the twelve disciples too. Theologians argue that the number twelve is significant in a religious context. There were twelve tribes of Israel and it is hypothesised that each disciple was a symbolic leader of each of the tribes and that the disciples represented the New Israel. This may or may not be true but there is another, more pragmatic reason why there were twelve disciples – it is a manageable number. The group is large enough to offer significant personnel resource but small enough to allow a relationship with every member of the twelve.

Team Selection

Although there is little detail about the disciples in the gospels, we can still ascertain elements of Jesus' recruitment criteria. Clearly all of his disciples were men and this was a reflection of attitudes at the time. Preaching doctrine was considered the domain of men and so for Jesus to recruit women as his agents would simply not have worked.

The first four disciples were Simon (who he renamed Peter) and his brother Andrew; the brothers James and John (who he nicknamed Boanerges, 'Sons of Thunder'). They were all Galilean fishermen. The remaining eight consisted of Philip and Bartholomew; Matthew the tax collector and Thomas the twin; James, Thaddeus; Simon called Zealot and Judas Iscariot who would ultimately betray Jesus.

The descriptive names given to the last two are intriguing. What was Jesus doing with a Zealot in his inner group? The Zealots, a fanatical band of freedom fighters seeking independence from Rome, were notorious for mounting terrorist campaigns against the Roman occupiers in the first century AD. When they were faced with defeat by the Romans in 73 AD as they defended their last stronghold, Masada, the erstwhile palace of King HerodKing Herod, they committed mass suicide rather that be taken by the Romans. In all over a thousand men, women and children took their own lives. The Zealots were radical and resolved to violent use of force. A supporter of this extreme nationalist sect would seem to sit uncomfortably with Jesus' moral crusade.

Judas 'Iscariot' is another oddity. It is a strong possibility that his name "Iscariot" came from his membership of a band of brigands called *sciarii*. Contemporary historian Jospehus states in his book Jewish War: *"Their favourite trick was to mingle with festival crowds concealing under their garments small daggers with which they stabbed opponents. When their victims fell the assassins melted into the indignant crowd, and through their plausibility entirely defied detection. First to have his throat cut by them was Jonathan the High Priest and after him many were murdered every day."* Again, such a ruthless bandit did not appear to fit well with Jesus' message of forgiveness and compassion.

The inclusion of Matthew the tax collector raises eyebrows too. Tax collectors were servants of the Romans and were despised for handing over hard earned income to the hated occupiers. They were blamed for inflicting misery on ordinary people who struggled to make a living.

Jesus' inclusion of such people in his close band of followers seems contradictory. Their own backgrounds and lifestyles contradicted his message and ideology – but he appointed them all the same. One explanation is that he wanted a varied group to represent him. By welcoming different types he broadened his appeal. His philosophy was for all the peoples not just a select few. By having an inclusive policy he demonstrated that everyone was welcome.

The Value of Loyalty

Another explanation is that Jesus was not interested in people's past. Jesus' whole philosophy was one of offering people a fresh start and of wiping the slate clean. That meant that individuals were welcome into the group provided that they made a personal commitment to him. Jesus was not looking for a 'type' – he was looking for loyalty. If they devoted themselves to him – they were good enough. The embracing nature of Jesus has attracted many people to Christianity both in his lifetime and down through the centuries. Even the most unworthy felt they could find solace and acceptance in his 'Kingdom'.

Nevertheless, it was a brave selection procedure for a man who preached a new moral code. The company he kept made him an easy target for his enemies. He had to suffer snide remarks and vicious slights and was frequently criticised for mixing with the unclean, the unworthy, sinners, tax collectors and women of dubious repute. But Jesus was steadfastly loyal to his followers which in itself inspired incredible loyalty from them in return. The depth of that loyalty can be measured by the fact that hundreds of followers were prepared to die rather than denounce him during the years of persecution after his death.

Close friends

He treated the Twelve almost as family. There was a revealing incident when someone shouted to Jesus that his mother and brothers were looking to talk to him and he replied *"Who is my mother? And who are my brethren?"* And then in a magnanimous gesture to his disciples he spread his arms wide and said: *"Behold my mother and my brethren!"* (Luke 12:49). His high regard for his followers is clear but he demanded reciprocal commitment in return:

> *"He that loveth father or mother more than me is not worthy of me: and he that loveth son or daughter more than me is not worthy of me." (Matthew 10:37)*

Tier 4 – Approved Sales Force

As Jesus' fame and notoriety grew, it became ever more difficult to handle the demand for his message. A kind of 'Jesus mania' had gripped Galilee and the surrounding regions. In response Jesus appointed a further seventy followers to represent him officially (Luke 10:1). They functioned as a second level sales force which kept the momentum of his movement going.

Little else is known of the seventy other than that they were sent on a mission to spread the good news. These followers had a functional rather than pivotal role in Jesus' organisation.

Tier 5 – All Other Followers

The criterion for becoming a follower was simple enough – they simply had to be totally committed to his cause. He had no time for slackers, or fly-by-nights. He told them that if they were not prepared to forgo their families, children, spouses and even their own lives, then they could not be a follower. He asked prospective followers to think long and hard before following him because the going would get tough.

> *"For which of you, intending to build a tower, sitteth not down first, and counteth the cost, whether he have sufficient to finish it? Lest haply, after he hath laid the foundation, and is not able to finish it, all that behold it begin to mock him, Saying, 'This man began to build, and was not able to finish.'" (Luke 14:28-30)*

His message was crystal clear – don't start if you can't finish!

His approach acted as an amazingly effective recruitment filter. By expounding on the difficulties and the extent of sacrifices that were required, Jesus made people think hard before joining him. Those that did formed a highly dedicated team which was prepared to make the ultimate sacrifice for the cause.

Critical Mass

Despite Jesus' demanding criteria for following him, thousands did. The sheer number of followers he attracted gave his movement critical mass. Each follower was charged with the responsibility of proselytising and bringing more people into the 'kingdom'. By adopting an inclusive policy to sales, he had effectively created a sales force of many thousands.

Wisdom of Jesus

1. **Organise teams into manageable groups. Jesus divided his followers into four tiers below himself. Three very close friends; a specially selected twelve disciples; an associate group of seventy and then his followers in general.**

2. **If you are the leader – lead. Jesus did not run his organisation as a democracy.**

3. **Accept your superior position in a business hierarchical context but treat those who report to you at all times with fairness, humanity and respect.**

4. **Form an inner team of individuals which might be capable of taking over when you leave.**

5. **Ensure the individuals have compatible personalities to yourself. You will be working closely with them.**

6. **Select individuals who are passionate about the cause you champion.**

7. **Only bring people that can be trusted into the inner team.**

8. **Use them for support – if necessary on an emotional as well as on a business level.**

9. **If broad appeal is an objective then allow many different types of people to act as agents.**

10. **Pick a manageable number for your lead sales team. Sufficient numbers to be a significant human resource but few enough to form real relationships with each one of them.**

11. **Let loyalty to you and your objectives be the biggest deciding factor on recruiting to the lead sales team.**

12. **View your top sales team almost as family.**

13. **Demand total commitment from the outset. Outline the sacrifices required to execute the job well. Make sure that potential recruits have thought through all the consequences before committing. This approach leads to a lower staff turnover and higher dedication to you and the team.**

14. **Be loyal to your team.**

15. **Demand absolute loyalty in return.**

16. **Be prepared to pull in more resource at short notice to keep the momentum of your campaign going.**

15

Training the Team

The process by which the disciples graduated to become fully fledged 'authorised' representatives of Jesus was organised, thorough and sophisticated. Jesus trained and taught them on an on-going basis until he was satisfied of their ability to communicate his message. As their leader he took a holistic view to training and dealt with their whole requirements. He taught them his ideology; answered their questions; dealt with their concerns; prepared them for conflict; motivated them and took care of their welfare. He was more than just a classroom teacher – he was their mentor and guardian. His training methods managed to turn a group of unremarkable men into a sales force capable of igniting the whole Roman Empire.

Jesus used eight principles to stunning effect – his first one was to let them know just who was the boss!

1. Establish Leadership

From what we know of Jesus we can ascertain that he was forthright, a man of destiny and a man who led rather than followed. It comes as no surprise, therefore, that from the start Jesus laid down the ground rules of his relationship with his disciples – he was their leader, they were his apprentices. In Matthew, after he called his disciples to him he warned:

> *The disciple is not above his master, nor the servant above his lord. (Matthew 10:24)*

Having got the pecking order straight he set them an exacting target – to be like him!

> *It is enough for the disciple that he be as his master, and the servant as his lord. (Matthew 10:25)*

Luke stated the master – apprentice relationship even more succinctly:

> *The disciple is not above his master: but every one that is perfect shall be as his master. (Luke 6:40)*

Jesus could not have put it more clearly. Firstly, he was in charge and secondly, the ultimate aim of the disciples is to be exactly like himself. Indeed, only when a person is 'as his master' do they reach perfection. This was the basis of Jesus' whole approach to training. By imparting knowledge, by constantly monitoring and by setting an example, Jesus intended to mould the disciples into his own image. He wanted them to think like him, work like him, behave like him. By being like him, Jesus could have confidence in their ability to propagate his message to the world.

Towards the end of his life, when Jesus was in Jerusalem, he altered the servant-master relationship to one based on friendship. By this time the disciples had in effect completed the course and he was ready to hand over the reins of his movement – his trainees had come of age.

> *"Henceforth I call you not servants; for the servant knoweth not what his lord doeth: but I have called you friends; for all things that I have heard of my Father I have made known unto you." (John 15:15)*

The disciples had been trained and now understood their master's 'business'. It was time to redress the relationship. As ever with Jesus, there were strings attached to the friendship. They could only call themselves his friends if they carried out his will!

> *"Ye are my friends, if ye do whatsoever I command you." (John 15:14)*

2. Lead from the Front

After this first lesson, Jesus' first act as their role model was to demonstrate the importance of spreading the message:

> *And it came to pass, when Jesus had made an end of commanding his twelve disciples, he departed thence to teach and to preach in their cities. (Matthew 11:1)*

Through actions as much as words the disciples learnt that the number one priority was to spread the message. Jesus' aim was to turn his disciples into a crack team of preachers who could spread his message far and wide. This was not going to happen overnight. He recognised that he needed to invest a huge amount of time and effort in order to lift the standard of his team to a level where they would be an effective sales force.

3. Make Time for your Team

Initially the disciples were a disparate group of individuals from widely different backgrounds. They held different beliefs, both religious and political, and had different sets of values. They were of different intellectual capabilities and some would make better communicators than others. He needed to work on these men before they would be ready to represent him and that meant making time for them. Time was needed to explain his ideology; how to spread the message; what ambitions he had for them; and what difficulties lay ahead. The scriptures refer many times to occasions when Jesus took his disciples aside for private tuition:

> *And Jesus going up to Jerusalem took the twelve disciples apart in the way. (Matthew 20:17-18)*
>
> *And when he was alone, they that were about him with the twelve asked of him the parable. (Mark 4:10)*
>
> *......and when they were alone, he expounded all things to his disciples. (Mark 4:34)*
>
> *He answered and said unto them, "Because it is given unto you to know the mysteries of the kingdom of heaven, but to them it is not given." (Matthew 13:11)*

A picture emerges of a leader who put enormous value on the time he spent with his apprentices. He believed in holding private sessions away from the distractions of day to day issues. Quietness and privacy provided the environment in which the disciples could freely ask questions and allow Jesus ample time to give thorough answers.

4. Empowering

The disciples were not at liberty to preach or carry out important ministry work unless they had Jesus' express permission. First of all they had to earn the right to represent Jesus' sect and only Jesus could give them that authority and power. Early in Mark's Gospel he actually conducted a rite in which he appointed the disciples and revealed to them that their ultimate purpose was to preach to all nations. The ceremony served to cement the relationship between Jesus and his disciples. He was their leader and they were his chosen team charged with the duty of spreading his message.

And he goeth up into a mountain, and calleth unto him whom he would: and they came unto him and he ordained twelve, that they should be with him, and that he might send them forth to preach. (Mark 3:13-14)

Jesus did not send them out to preach, however, until later when they had graduated to a position where he could place his trust in them. When they had reached this level Jesus conducted a special initiation ceremony in which he *gave them power and authority over all devils, and to cure disease*. (Luke 9:1) It was only then that he sent them on their first mission to complete their main task of preaching *the kingdom of God, and to heal the sick* (Luke 9:2).

5. In at the Shallow End

Jesus knew that spreading his message would be perilous for his novices. He compared their plight to being like lambs amongst wolves (Matthew 10:16)! His approach, therefore, was to put them in at the shallow end first. Plenty of time for the tough stuff later. On their first mission he told his disciples not to bother with the Samaritans, a neighbouring non-Jewish tribe but to concentrate on Jewish cities instead. This is the equivalent of asking them to stay with warm prospects, people who would at least listen to them and understand their proposition. You would not send a new, wet behind the ears sales executive to sell to the coldest, meanest prospects – Jesus would not either. He was acutely aware of the damage early knock-backs would have on the fragile confidence of his sales team. The more exacting prospects would come later.

These twelve Jesus sent forth, and commanded them, saying, "Go not into the way of the Gentiles, and into any city of the Samaritans enter ye not: But go rather to the lost sheep of the house of Israel. And as ye go, preach, saying, 'The kingdom of heaven is at hand'." (Matthew 10:5-7)

6. Set High Targets

Despite his frustrations and the limitations of his disciples, Jesus never lost faith in them. If anything he set them extremely high targets. He told them that they were privileged and that the knowledge they had was like having a light which they could share with others:

> *"No man, when he hath lighted a candle, covereth it with a vessel, or putteth it under a bed; but setteth it on a candlestick, that they which enter in may see the light." (Luke 8:16)*

Moreover he instructed them to take this light to the whole world. He envisaged them being able to achieve things which he himself would not be able to do. He instructed them that *the gospel must first be published among all nations* (Mark 13:10), and that they would take it to the very highest echelons within each country. Indeed, he expected them to stand witness to his message before governors and kings (Mark 13:9). It is a mark of Jesus' superb training techniques and motivational prowess that after his death they went on to do just that.

7. Strong Work Ethic

The disciples learnt that Jesus was a hard task master. He set high standards and demanded total commitment from his disciples. He never, however, asked them to do anything he was not prepared to do himself. As their role model he was totally unforgiving on himself. He worked relentlessly for his cause and the disciples quickly came to appreciate that Jesus led from the front.

In John's gospel we learn that Jesus was so busy baptising, the special initiation rite whereby people who were immersed in a pool of water were reborn into the 'Kingdom of God', that he was doing more baptisms that the eponymous John The Baptist (who was evidently famous for baptising). The author of that gospel then mentions in passing *Though Jesus himself baptised not, but his disciples* (John 4:2). It would seem that Jesus was so successful in attracting conversions into the 'Kingdom' that he needed his disciples to 'process the orders'.

There was a strong work ethic amongst the disciples who were frequently required to 'muck in' and help out in day to day activities. They were sent ahead to prepare for his entries into towns; rowed the boats that he travelled in, and ran errands for him. On several occasions it is recorded that the disciples distributed food among thousands of people and then were responsible for collecting the scraps – an arduous and mundane task. Living with Jesus was not an easy life – there was no room for the uncommitted or feint-hearted. Jesus worked them hard for his cause.

8. Feedback

An essential part of the training process was to obtain feedback from the disciples. In this way he could monitor their progress and put right any difficulties they might have. After the disciples had been out on a preaching mission, the disciples returned and reported to Jesus. It is a classic training technique. They expounded on their experiences, Jesus would guide, comment and encourage. By constantly working with his team he perfected his selling machine.

> *And the apostles gathered themselves together unto Jesus and told him all things, both what they had done, and what they had taught. (Mark 6:30)*

> *And the apostles, when they were returned, told him all that they had done. And he took them, and went aside privately into a desert place belonging to the city called Bethsaida (Luke 9:10)*

Jesus held the debrief in a quiet place so that he could learn of their endeavours, instruct and advise without distraction.

A Trainer's Frustration

Jesus knew it was going to be a long haul to build his team up to standard. He himself was a learned man, fully versed in Judaism and knowledgeable of current affairs. Many of his disciples were from humble backgrounds. Education was not universal and boys who went into the fishing trade, for instance may have joined their fathers at work from a very young age. The technicalities of Jesus' new Kingdom, therefore, often escaped many of them.

There was one occasion which was almost comical in the extent of misunderstanding. Jesus had warned the disciples to be cautious of the 'leaven' bread of the Pharisees and King HerodKing Herod's men. By leaven bread he was actually referring to the way of life of the above groups. Admittedly the utterance is a little cryptic but the mundane spin that the disciples put on the comment was pure bathos. They thought he was referring to fact that they had run out of bread! Jesus was incensed. After all the miraculous deeds he was credited with, after all he had achieved, why on earth would he warn them that they were running out of bread? Jesus rebuked them for their stupidity:

> *......and when Jesus knew it, he saith unto them, "Why reason ye, because ye have no bread? Perceive ye not yet, neither understand? Have ye your heart yet hardened? Having eyes, see ye not? And having ears, hear ye not? And do ye not remember? When I brake the five loaves among five thousand, how many baskets full of fragments took ye up?" They say unto him, "Twelve." "And when the seven among four thousand, how many baskets full of fragments took ye up?" And they said, "Seven." And he said unto them, "How is it that ye do not understand?" (Mark 8:17-21)*

This very human incident of a frustrated teacher irked by the slowness of his rather dim pupils finds resonance today in classrooms everywhere. Unfortunately Jesus' propensity to vent his irritation if they failed to grasp his meaning meant that the disciples were not always forthcoming with matters they did not understand.

But they understood not that saying, and were afraid to ask him. (Mark 9:32)

The slowness of the disciples might explain Jesus' habit of talking to them in parables, a technique he used many times to explain complex issues through stories or everyday parallels.

The Wisdom of Jesus

1. **From the outset establish who is in charge.**

2. **Establish the leader as a role model that they should aspire to.**

3. **As a leader, lead by example – never ask your trainees to do something you yourself are not prepared to do.**

4. **Set aside time for the training of your team.**

5. **Hold training sessions in private and quietness – away from day to day distractions.**

6. **Empower trainees by recognising their success. This might involve a special graduation ceremony.**

7. **Start trainees off with less difficult tasks allowing confidence to grow. More exacting challenges can come later.**

8. **Set high standards. They might get there!**

9. **Establish a strong work ethic. Use your team to relieve workload whenever necessary.**

10. **Obtain feedback from the trainees. This way their progress can be monitored and problems can be addressed.**

11. **Even if you become frustrated with your trainees, avoid castigating them. A severe reprimand will discourage them from confiding in you when other difficulties arise.**

16

Team Welfare, Morale and Motivation: The 10 Golden Rules

Winston Churchill's proclaimed on the occasion of eightieth birthday in 1954: "I have never accepted what many people have kindly said, namely that I inspired a nation. It was the nation and the race dwelling all round the globe that had the lion heart. I had the luck to be called upon to give the roar." He was of course being far too modest. Churchill ranks as one of the greatest and most inspirational leaders of the modern era.

For all his great qualities he is perhaps best remembered for his indomitable 'bulldog spirit' and as an accomplished orator. His great wartime speeches (which include the unforgettable "we shall fight you on the beaches"; "never in the field of conflict" and "blood, sweat and tears" addresses) gripped wartime Britain. Through them he articulated the peril facing his country; united it against the common enemy and galvanised it to seek "victory at all costs". His ability to empathise as well as offer hope and encouragement lifted the morale of the whole nation. Indubitably, his skills as a communicator helped guide Britain through its darkest days and onwards to victory. Jesus had the same morale-boosting effect on his followers.

Like wartime Britons, the disciples were inspired and prepared to face all manner of hardship, including death, in a cause they fervently believed in. It is sobering to consider that despite all Jesus had done in his lifetime, Christianity could never have taken a hold without the determination of the disciples to continue to spread his message after his demise. How Jesus managed to motivate his band of followers was of critical importance to the success of his long term strategy. Here we outline the ten golden principles Jesus used to inspire the disciples to go on to change the world.

1. Building Confidence

Even if Jesus' message was heaven sent, his feet remained firmly on the ground. He never allowed his divine ambition to blind him to the needs of those around him. More than anyone he was aware that his followers were required to make incredible sacrifices in order to follow him. He effectively asked them to leave the security of their normal lives and follow him into an uncertain future. He expected them to leave their families, friends, homes and work. He even warned them that to follow him was fraught with danger. Such big upheavals in people's lives leads to anxiety, stress and insecurity. Jesus was wise to the potential crises in confidence and took pains to assure them of the wisdom of their decision:

> *"Whosoever cometh to me, and heareth my sayings, and doeth them, I will show you to whom he is like: He is like a man which built an house, and digged deep and laid the foundation on a rock: and when the flood arose, the stream beat vehemently upon that house, and could not shake it: for it was founded upon a rock." (Luke 6:47-48)*

Jesus turned accepted wisdom on its head. He claimed that by following him (which must have seemed a high risk venture to most) his disciples would be building on solid foundations. He promised that by listening to his sayings and acting on them they would be safe from the trials and tribulations that life would throw at them. Even if his promise was intended on a spiritual level it would have been the kind of reassurance that the disciples needed at the outset of their adventure with Jesus.

2. Reassurance

Knowing the sacrifices that his disciples were required to make made it imperative that they felt valued. To treat them in any other way risked disloyal and disaffected followers – not the sort he could entrust to convert the known world to Christianity. Jesus claimed that in his new 'Kingdom' his followers were of immense value and concern to God himself. He drew parallels with nature to powerfully underline the extent of their value.

> *"Are not five sparrows sold for two farthings, and not one of them is forgotten before God? But even the very hairs of your head are all numbered. Fear not therefore: ye are of more value than many sparrows." (Luke 12:6-7)*

> *"Consider the ravens: for they neither sow nor reap; which neither have storehouse nor barn; and God feedeth them: how much more are ye better than the fowls? And which of you with taking thought can add to his stature one cubit? If ye then be not able to do that thing which is least, why take ye thought for the rest? Consider the lilies how they grow: they toil not, they spin not; and yet I say unto you, that Solomon in all his glory was not arrayed like one of these. If then God so clothe the grass, which is to day in the field, and to morrow is cast into the oven; how much more will he clothe you, O ye of little faith?" (Luke 12:24-28)*

The comparisons were elegant, memorable and uplifting. Jesus allayed fears and smoothed anxieties away, leaving his disciples free to concentrate on building the 'Kingdom'. Through his warm words he built their confidence and egos.

3. Privilege

Motivated people value and believe in the cause they espouse (be it selling insurance policies or spreading the gospel). Jesus fostered positive attitudes to his cause by proclaiming they were in a privileged position. In private he told them that they were fortunate to be his followers.

> *And he turned him unto his disciples, and said privately, "Blessed are the eyes which see the things that ye." (Luke 10:23)*

At other times he treated them as his confidantes. They were privy to information and explanations that he would not disclose to the masses. In essence they were part of an 'in crowd' – privileged insiders who received special treatment.

> *He answered and said unto them, "Because it is given unto you to know the mysteries of the kingdom of heaven, but to them it is not given." (Matthew 13:11)*

He urged them to value the lessons he taught. He told them that his teachings were like having precious stones. Jesus could not offer his followers money but he gave them 'treasure' of another kind instead (Matthew 13:52). Jesus never shied away from letting his disciples know just how fortunate they were.

4. Motivation – Carrots and Sticks

Jesus was prepared to offer conditional incentives to his disciples. He told his men that if they spread the message to the people, he would endorse them before God. As the disciples believed him to be a prophet or even the Messiah himself this was a wonderful offer. Through him they could gain access to the Almighty!

> *"Also I say unto you, Whosoever shall confess me before men, him*

shall the Son of man also confess before the angels of God." (Luke 12:7)

The deal, however, was two edged!

"But he that denieth me before men shall be denied before the angels of God." (Luke 12:8)

Having offered a carrot he threatened a stick – if they did not deliver he would disown them in front of God.

Modern day scenarios abound. In sales, for instance, the same ploy is often used to motivate sales people. A sales director might announce to his sales staff that if they hit the month's sales targets then he will have a word on their behalf with the boss. For many of the staff who do not have access to the top, this is a fantastic opportunity to gain recognition. Will they try and hit those sales targets? Of course they will!

But like Jesus the sales director could take it a stage further and also add that if any staff fail to hit their minimum targets then they will need to make an appointment to talk to him about the situation. This may seem a bit drastic – but very effective!

Psychologists debate as to whether the desire to succeed is a bigger motivational factor than the fear of failure. It is probably the case that different people are motivated in different measures by both conditions. Jesus did not leave it to chance – he used both – the sweetness of success mixed with the bitter taste of failure. With a big carrot in front of them and a large stick behind them, the only way was forward.

5. Focus – Prepare the Team for Hardship

When Winston Churchill became Prime Minister in May 1940 he announced: "I have nothing to offer but blood, toil, tears and sweat." It seemed a harsh message for a nation already reeling from Hitler's onslaught. But Churchill saw no point in offering glib platitudes or belittling the task ahead. He told the nation straight and the nation responded with an unprecedented effort.

Similarly, Jesus knew of the severe difficulties ahead for his followers. Preaching in the hothouse atmosphere of ancient Israel was a hazardous occupation. Israel housed many different factions and sects. To be outspoken was to make enemies as Jesus knew from bitter experience. He was aware of the dangers and the shark-like predators that awaited his naive and inexperienced followers. He warned them of trouble ahead – forewarned is forearmed.

> *"Behold, I send you forth as sheep in the midst of wolves: be ye therefore wise as serpents, and harmless as doves." (Matthew 10:16)*

This analogy must have terrified his novices. Implicit in his warning is that they would find themselves in perilous situations – even mortal danger. Jesus was very concerned, therefore, that his disciples avoid trouble whenever possible. His advice is to be wise, smart, and cool. He told them to keep their wits about them and advised against hot-headed overreaction. He encouraged a passive stance when confronted with a dangerous situation. He noticeably did not encourage them to fight back or engage in head to head conflict. This would have been antagonistic and would probably have left the inexperienced disciples worse off for the encounter.

Jesus' stern warning would also have had a wonderful effect on concentrating his disciples' minds. Jesus was making clear that to follow him was a serious undertaking and involved real peril. If the disciples were going to deal with the dangers ahead they needed to be keen, attentive and obedient.

6. Crisis Management Skills

Jesus could not protect them for ever and there would come a time when they would find themselves in hot water. In such a situation, Jesus told them not to worry about what they should say. The words would come to them![13]

> *But when they deliver you up, take no thought how or what ye shall speak: for it shall be given you in that same hour what ye shall speak. (Matthew 10:19)*

Jesus was confident that their training would see them through. We have seen that Jesus himself was consummate at dealing with adversaries – never at a loss for words. Through training them he believed that they too would be capable of handling even the most difficult of inquisitors. But this level of competence would take time.

There was an occasion when some of his disciples were being hassled by some baleful scribes while Jesus, Peter, James and John were away up a high mountain (Mark 9:14). When Jesus came down and saw his disciples ensnared in an argument, he immediately took control of the situation and demanded to know what questions the scribes were badgering his men with. His reaction was borne of a protective instinct towards his disciples and a realisation that they were not then ready to take on the wily scribes who schemed to embarrass and discredit all those involved with his movement.

7. Teamwork

Jesus realised that even though he claimed he would be with his disciples on a spiritual level – selling is a lonely and often thankless task. It takes perseverance, dedication and a thick hide. Even the best sales people hit bad patches – they lose form; sales dry up; luck conspires against them. In such circumstances it easy to become despondent and negative and this of course affects the sales process. Sales dip even further and depression sets in. To counter this process Jesus sent his disciples out with a partner or 'sales buddy'. Two people can work together and provide mutual support and friendship. When one gets down the other works to pick him or her up. By sending out teams he had a more effective and resilient sales force.

> *After these things the Lord appointed other seventy also, and sent them two and two before his face into every city any place, whither he himself would come. (Luke 10:1)*

And he called unto him the twelve, and began to send them forth by two and two; and gave them power over unclean spirits. (Mark 6:7)

8. Team Welfare

As part of Jesus' all encompassing approach to training, Jesus took interest in the welfare of his trainees. Not unnaturally, given the ferocious pace that Jesus set, they sometimes became weary and hungry. When this happened he knew it was time to stop:

> *And he said unto them, "Come ye yourselves apart into a desert place, and rest a while," for there were many coming and going and they had no leisure so much as to eat. And they departed into a desert place by ship privately. (Mark 6:31-32).*

As well as being necessary, the rest was awarded as a recognition of hard work. Jesus had a well rounded and progressive attitude to man management. He was a demanding task master but always ensured that his men were in good shape to deliver. Exhausted and hungry people are unfit to handle the stresses and strains that life throws at them, never mind lessons on the 'Kingdom'.

As we have already seen, one of the first disputes Jesus had with the authorities was when his followers ate corn as they passed through a field on the Sabbath (which was considered to be work and, therefore, not permitted as the Sabbath is a day of rest). When he was cross-examined about this behaviour he defended his disciples' actions by stating that the Sabbath was made for man, not the other way round. For Jesus, his men's hunger was more important than a technical law.

Likewise, a sales person who has been out on the road all week would respond positively to a boss who offers some respite with a quiet drink or a relaxing dinner. Such simple acts of consideration develop loyalty, respect and commitment – as well as revitalising an important part of your team. It costs little and is hugely effective. Jesus was a supreme man manager.

9. Bonding

Jesus was host to the Last Supper, the most famous meal of all time. This dinner with his twelve closest followers is steeped in religious symbolism and meaning. Even today millions of Christians re-enact the event daily. Many theologians believe that this supper was the starting point of Christianity. Before this event it is argued that Jesus and his followers considered themselves to be essentially Jewish. At the supper, however, Jesus broke away from tradition and instructed his disciples to conduct the Passover meal in his name – thereby providing a new focus for the ritual and establishing an entirely new religion.

Whatever the theological implications of this highly charged meal, we can infer that he placed great importance on sharing food and drink with his closest friends and followers. He valued the privacy and intimacy the occasion afforded and, aware that his arrest was imminent, chose to spend some of the few hours he had left with them in this manner.

> *And he said unto them, "With desire I have desired to eat this Passover with you before I suffer. For I say unto you, I will not any more eat thereof, until it be fulfilled in the kingdom of God." And he took the cup, and gave thanks, and said, "Take this, and divide it among yourselves: For I say unto you, I will not drink of the fruit of the vine, until the Kingdom of God shall come." And he took bread, and gave thanks, and brake it, and gave unto them, saying, "This is my body which is given for you: this do in remembrance of me." Likewise also the cup after supper, saying, "This cup is the new testament in my blood, which is shed for you." (Luke 22:15-20)*

10. Highlight the Ultimate Reward

While Jesus was open about the difficulties that lay ahead, he also highlighted the benefits of enduring to the end:

And ye shall be hated of all men for my name's sake: but he that endureth to the end shall be saved. (Matthew 10:22)

Jesus approach was to steel them for hardship whilst simultaneously reassure them of their ultimate reward. He built up their self esteem; assured them of their own self-worth and incentivised them by offering them salvation for enduring the hardship. His method worked. His disciples were enthusiastic, dedicated and spectacularly effective. The world we live in today would not be the same if they had not been.

The Wisdom of Jesus

1. **Reassure trainees that they have made the right decision in investing in your cause.**
2. **Make a concerted effort to reassure them that you have their best interests at heart.**
3. **Confide in your apprentices – make them feel part of an inner team.**
4. **Stress the privilege it is to be part of the team and have the opportunity to learn.**
5. **Stress that the information and training they receive is like gold dust – rare and valuable.**
6. **Incentivise your team by promising to further their careers if successful.**
7. **On the flip side, let it be known that poor performances will not be tolerated.**
8. **If trainees are likely to encounter aggressive adversaries, advise them to stay alert to the danger and avoid hot-headed over reaction.**
9. **Give trainees fair warning of any dangers and difficulties ahead – it concentrates their minds.**
10. **In the event that the trainees do find themselves in a difficult situation, reassure them that their training will see them through.**
11. **Allocate each sales person a 'sales buddy' for mutual sup-**

port and friendship. Teams are more effective and resilient than lone individuals.

12. **Be responsible for their welfare – tired, distressed or hungry trainees can not perform.**

13. **Take time to bond with your team. The sharing of food and drink is a special human occasion which strengthens the bonds between people.**

14. **Highlight the benefits of enduring the hardships and lasting the course.**

PART 4

IN CONCLUSION

17

Results

The world is gone after him. (John 12:19)

Any marketing campaign should be judged by results. It is one of the delights of marketing that it yields such tangible conclusions. Success or failure is easily discerned. Modern day marketers can judge success by the increase (or otherwise) of sales. In the case of more ethereal activities such as building awareness or changing attitudes, they can measure success by conducting pre- and post-campaign research analysis. If a positive shift in awareness or attitudes is detected, then a commensurate level of success has been attained.

We can measure the success of Jesus' campaigning by similar yardsticks: sales – the numbers of converts he won over to his cause; and awareness – the number of people who became aware of him and his doctrine. In the case of Jesus, we do not have to conduct pre-campaign analysis, because awareness of him was zero. He was a complete unknown from an unremarkable town, located in a little known region called Galilee. Jesus started from scratch.

Any marketer will tell you that new product launches are extremely hazardous. The consumer has to be coerced to trial your new offering. He or she then compares your offering with their old product and then consequently decides whether to switch their allegiance. It sounds deceptively easy but there are three major obstacles in the way. Firstly, awareness has to be built so that people know of your product or service. This process takes tremendous resource and application. Secondly, you have to break the established purchasing habits of your target audience. These are often ingrained and are literally habits of a lifetime. Thirdly, your competition will not take it lying down. They will use every tactic at their disposal to scupper your launch. Only one in forty new product ideas ever becomes a successful commercial product.

Any success Jesus enjoyed must be considered to be particularly remarkable. He was not offering an easy option. On the contrary, he offered a lifestyle which involved a degree of self-sacrifice and was, especially in his time, perilous. Many early Christians were persecuted and even killed because they chose to follow him.

Jesus also had to contend with a formidable 'competitor' – Judaism. This religion is not just a way of worship, it is a way of life. It pervades all aspects of Jewish life: work, rest, cleanliness, and religious practice. Much of what a Jew must abide by is defined down to the tiniest detail. There are for instance complex rituals surrounding food and the containers they were served in. Certain foods are deemed unclean (such as pork), and other foods and containers could become unclean by coming into contact with a dead body or a menstruating woman. It is worth reading some of laws contained within the scriptures to appreciate the scale of commitment that is required from practising Jews[14].

The Jews are and were passionate about their religion. Unlike the religions of their neighbours, they were monotheistic – they believed in one, mighty, all-powerful god – a god who was vengeful and jealous of all other gods[15]. He was not a god to be crossed lightly. Coercing Jews to forsake their religion was an awesome task.

Jesus avoided taking Judaism head on. He himself was a Jew and did not despise his religion. On the contrary, he treasured it and believed it was the immutable truth of God. Jesus' approach was to offer himself as the completion and continuance of Judaism, not a separate alternative.

Going for Growth

In this chapter we assess the results of his campaign and the expansion of Christianity as he journeyed from being an unknown son of a carpenter to the founder of a world-changing religion.

Galilean Ministry

His Galilean ministry was characterised by four inter-linked and sometimes overlapping phases:

- Endorsement from John the Baptist
- Recruitment and training of the disciples
- Campaigning throughout the region
- Verbal warfare with the authorities

Phase 1 – Endorsement

By receiving the unconditional endorsement from John the Baptist, Jesus received the perfect start to his campaign. The 'Baptiser' had his own set of disciples and followers and as such was a man of considerable influence. With John's full support, Jesus had a solid foundation on which to build his own credentials. He was now a name – someone worth listening to.

Phase 2 – Recruitment and Training

First on Jesus' agenda on returning to Galilee from seeing John, was to recruit and train helpers to spread the word. He famously called these men 'fishers of men'. They provided personnel on the ground to execute his strategy. The task was simply too vast for one man to complete on his own and, furthermore, he needed personnel to carry on his work after his death.

Phase 3 – The Campaign Trail

Bolstered by his newly appointed team, it was not long before Jesus made his mark. Mark reports that following the exorcism of an evil spirit in Capernaum Synagogue, word of him spread throughout Galilee:

And immediately his fame spread abroad throughout all the region round about Galilee. (Mark 1:28)

It was the start of a remarkable campaign which travelled at breakneck speed. The crowds became a common feature throughout Jesus' campaigning in Galilee. Wherever he went, crowds followed him. They grew so large that it actually became difficult to reach him. Mark tells a touching story of a group of resourceful men who were trying to carry their paralytic friend to Jesus who was in a building in Capernaum. Unfortunately, they could not reach him, as there was no room to reach him, even outside the door. They then had the innovative idea of clambering onto the roof and lowering their friend down into the building.

And when they could not come nigh unto him for the press they uncovered the roof where he was: and when they had broken it up they let down the bed wherein the sick of the palsy lay. (Mark 2:4)

Jesus continued to preach throughout Galilee but, such was his impact, news of him spread beyond the boundaries of the region.

And his fame went throughout all Syria (Matthew 4:24)

And there followed him great multitudes of people from Galilee, and from Decapolis, and from Jerusalem, and from Judaea, and from beyond Jordan (Matthew 4:25)

Jesus was building an international reputation.

Soon Jesus was sending out his disciples to preach on his behalf. This added further impetus to his fast moving campaign. The disciples made a tremendous impact which even King HerodKing Herod became aware of.

> *And King HerodKing Herod heard of him; (for his name was spread abroad) (Mark 6:14)*

By the time the disciples had returned from their first mission, the campaign had turned into an unstoppable bandwagon. Even when Jesus and his disciples sought some solitude out in the desert the crowds followed them.

> *And the people saw them departing, and many knew him, and ran afoot thither out of all cities, and outwent them, and came together unto him. (Mark 6:33)*

Once he had to deal with the logistics of feeding *about five thousand men, beside women and children* (Matthew 14:21). As woman and children were not included in this number, we can safely put the total number in attendance at many thousands more. On another occasion, he fed four thousand men (not including women and children). Drawing such massive numbers of people out to remote areas was a spectacular achievement. Jesus was a superstar and the crowds were on the verge of becoming unmanageable. They would pursue him from all over the region. Wherever he appeared, they carried their sick on stretchers and laid them on the street.

> *And when they were come out of the ship, straightway they knew him, and ran through that whole region round about, and began to carry about in beds those that were sick, where they heard he was. And whithersoever he entered, into villages, or cities or country, they laid the sick in the streets, and besought him that they might touch if it were but the border of his garment: and as many as touched him were made whole. (Mark 6:54-56).*

On one occasion, even his family could not reach him because of the multitude of people surrounding him (Luke 8:19). On another, the people were jammed so tightly together that they were treading on each others toes.

> *In the mean time, when there were gathered together an innumerable multitude of people, insomuch that they trode one upon another. (Luke 12:1)*

Jesus was a sensation and the crowds could not get enough of him.

Phase 4 – Conflict

The crowds were a big concern of the chief priests and Pharisees. They saw him as a threat to their own power base and as a destabilising influence likely to agitate the Romans who would think nothing of quashing any hint of insurrection in brutal fashion.

They tried a series of ruses devised either to catch Jesus out or to sully his reputation. But Jesus welcomed the challenge. He consistently humiliated the authorities. The crowd frequently made comparisons between Jesus' ability to teach *them as one that had authority* (Mark 1:22) and the lacklustre performance of the Pharisees. He never shied away from conflict and never attempted to resolve his differences with them behind closed doors. The conflict brought him valuable positive publicity. The crowds also afforded Jesus an element of protection. The authorities were evidently scared of the crowd reaction should they attempt to arrest him in front of them.

His running battle went all the way to Jerusalem where he played them like pawns to deliver his death sentence. It is ironic that it was the Pharisees, his biggest opponents who so desperately wanted to stop him, who forecast what was happening with such prescience:

> *The Pharisees therefore said among themselves, "Perceive ye how ye prevail nothing? Behold, the world is gone after him." (John 12:19)*

What happened next?

Jesus was executed on the orders of the Romans about 30 AD. Within seven weeks of his death, rumours were rife that he had risen from the dead and many thousands of Jews came to believe that he was alive and that his death was part of God's grand design to save mankind. The Church[16] had its origins about this time.

His disciples, who had been commissioned to *teach all nations* (Matthew 28:19), duly got down to business. The three years of intensive training and tuition from the master had turned them into a formidable sales force for Jesus. Within thirty years, Christianity had spread to most of the Eastern region of the Roman Empire and was moving inexorably towards Rome.

The centre of the Christian faith remained in Jerusalem where thousands were converted each year. From here it spread to Judaea and even Samaria where mass conversions took place amongst the despised Samaritans. Soon Christianity reached Cyprus and Antioch, the third city of the Roman Empire.

Peter, Jesus' friend, became head of the Church. For many years he remained in Jerusalem but following a vision which instructed him to take the message to the gentiles he set out from the capital. He ultimately ended up in Rome where he was killed in Nero's persecution of the Christians in about 64 AD. News of his martyrdom travelled throughout the Empire and inspired many new conversions to Christianity.

Peter also welcomed the work of a new convert called Paul. Paul had started out as being violently opposed to Christianity. Following his conversion, however, he became an astonishingly good evangelist visiting and corresponding with many communities throughout the region including the Greeks, Corinthians, Galations, Ephesians, Colossians, Philippians and Romans. He visited Rome twice and on his second visit was also killed in Nero's persecutions in 64 AD.

By the end of the first century, Christianity had churches as far west as Rome. By the end of the second century churches were established in France and North Africa. By the end of the third century there were Christian communities throughout the whole Roman Empire. By 363 AD Rome had its first Christian Emperor. The most powerful man in the world was a Christian. Christianity had grown into *a great tree; and the fowls of the air lodged in the branches of it.* (Luke 13:19).

Through the next fifteen centuries the pace of Christian expansion was relentless. Each new generation of Christians preach the message with the same amazing zeal as their predecessors – in the same way that the first disciples kept the flame alight after the crucifixion of Jesus.

By the twentieth century Christianity had grown from one man to reach all nations and claim one third of the world's population. He set out to have his message *published among all nations* and he did it. Mission accomplished.

Gathering Clouds

As we enter the new millennium, however, clouds have appeared on the horizon. His message will indubitably survive – but the established churches, hitherto the vehicle of his message, may not. It is possible we are seeing the beginning of a slow but terminal decline of organised Christian religion. What is happening in the UK is indicative of what is occurring in many western countries world-wide. Here it is predicted that by the millennium the number of adults attending Roman Catholic mass each week in the UK will fall to 973,000 compared with 1,600,000 in 1980. Meanwhile Anglican churches are predicted to attract only 832,000 down from 968,000 in 1980.[17] Clearly some churches are faring better than others but the decline is generally universal. Across all denominations it is estimated that church membership will have declined by 20% from 1980 to 2000.

These are grim times for established churches. While two thirds of the UK population still profess to believe in God most are not prepared to do anything about it. For many people religion is way down their list of priorities coming behind their careers, their children's education, payment of household bills, the upkeep of their house, where they will go on holiday and frankly who wins the big match on Saturday. In a world full of distractions, concerns and easy delights, religion is not faring well – but much of the church's recent demise is self inflicted.

The church generally has become increasingly introverted, lacking in confidence and unsure of its place in the world. Complacency and a lack of direction have set in. It no longer sets the agenda for debate and is increasingly irrelevant to the vast majority of people. It is becoming outdated and weak and a shadow of the robust movements which, with missionary zeal, set the world ablaze down through the centuries. At the current rate of contraction the church will find themselves talking to empty pews well before the next millennium is out.

Some church leaders have tried to stem the haemorrhaging . Initiatives include guitars in church to pep up Sunday service; the introduction of dance and drama groups; and inviting people in for tea and coffee – but the church is deluding itself if it believes it can stem a mass exodus by fiddling with the peripherals. The problem is more fundamental than that.

There is, however, an answer. And if the church wants to start to win its people back, it need look no further than the example set by its first champion.

In contrast to the modern day church, which has become largely passive and hesitant, Jesus was an aggressive marketer armed with a decisive strategy. He believed in taking his message to the people – wherever he could find them. The remote, laissez faire attitude of many churches today would be anathema to him. He trawled Israel and foreign countries for potential converts to his cause. He had an insatiable appetite for conversions and irrespective of whether he was accepted or rejected he continued his search for new prospects. He was energy personified, an unstoppable force.

From the outset he moved to centre stage and became the focal point for discussion. Seizing the moral high ground he set the agenda, provoked controversy and took on the authorities. He packaged his messages in a relevant and memorable way and was persistent and courageous in the marketing of his message. Not known for his diplomacy, he ruthlessly destroyed alternative philosophies and warned his followers against them. They in turn worked hard for his cause, and then, with a religious passion, went on to spread his message to all nations.

In this way he shook up the world.

If the church wants more than a walk on part at the following millennium it needs to take a long hard look at itself and learn to follow its leader once again.

The disciple is not above his master: but every one that is perfect shall be as his master (Luke 6:40)

18

Conclusion

Writing this book has been a thrilling voyage of revelation. One of the most satisfying aspects of writing it is that the management and marketing principles developed here are based principally on original scriptural texts rather than personal conjecture. Indeed, every principle described in this book is derived from the four gospels.

It has also been hugely rewarding to consider that by studying Jesus' marketing and management genius we receive a glimpse of how the mind of this extraordinary man worked. In the course of appraising him in this manner we gain a new perspective on his life's accomplishments. We have witnessed his single-minded pursuit of one clear objective; his application of a winning grand plan and his amazing attention to detail. We have analysed his techniques for building awareness, his total grasp of PR and the value he placed on endorsement. We have learnt of his stunning communication techniques including the use of parables, the wielding of authority and his clever use of sound bites. We have seen how he built a sales force to take his message to the world; how he motivated and offered incentives to them and how he trained them to sell his vision. Using these principles he took on the authorities, faced down the might of Rome, founded a new religion and established a new code of human morality that still stands strong today. And he did it all in just three years.

His life was a towering achievement. He, as much as anyone, has steered the course of mankind, leaving an indelible mark on all of our lives. We would all do well to take a moment to stop and consider *how* he ever managed to do it. I hope this book makes that task easier.

Bibliography

The following sources have proven invaluable in the writing of this book.

The King James Version of the Bible

The Holy Bible New International Version, Hodder & Stoughton Ltd (1995)

J. R. Porter, *The Illustrated Guide to the Bible,* Oxford University Press (1995)

A. N. Wilson, *Jesus,* Sinclair-Stevenson (1992)

Rex Nicholls & Patrick Vaughan, *The Gospel of Mark Illuminated,* Lion Publishing (1990)

The History of Christianity, Lion Publishing (1990)

John Bowker, *World Religions,* Dorling Kindersley (1997)

Sheila Wright, *Financial Times Marketing Casebook,* Pitman Publishing (1997)

Robert F. Hartley, *Marketing Mistakes and Successes*, John Wiley & Sons, Inc. (1998)

Andrew Sanger, *Explorer Israel,* AA Publishing (1996)

Oxford Companion to the Bible, Oxford University Press (1993)

Notes

1 Supreme religious council which resided in the temple area.

2 *Rejoice greatly, O daughter of Zion; shout, O daughter of Jerusalem: behold, thy King cometh unto thee: he is just, and having salvation; lowly, and riding upon an ass, and upon a colt the foal of an ass* (Zechariah 9:9)

3 Isaiah 56:7

4 Jeremiah 7:11

5 bowl

6 HerodKing Herod's wife was in fact already the wife of his brother Philip. Therefore the marriage was illegal under Judaic Law.

7 In the Old Testament book of Genesis, the cities of Sodom and Gomorrah were destroyed by God for their proclivity towards immoral and dissolute behaviour.

8 Isaiah 56:7

9 Jeremiah 7:11

10 Isaiah 29:13

11 Hosea 6:6

12 Matthew 17:1-13; Mark 9:2-12; Luke 9:28-36

13 The gospels actually state that the Holy Spirit would give them the words to answer adversaries. This might be true, but Jesus took no chances – he put an awful lot of effort into inculcating his message in their minds too!

14 Suggest reading Leviticus 23:3, 11:3-4, 8, 32-35, Exodus 20:8-11, Deuteronomy 14:3-21

15 Exodus 20:5 *Thou shalt not bow down thyself to them, nor serve them: for I the Lord thy God am a jealous God*

16 Church with a capital 'C' denotes the early Church founded by Jesus and his disciples. Church with a small 'c' is used as a generic term for all mainstream denominations of organized Christianity.

17 Source: UKCH Religious Trends 1998/1999.

Index